About the Auth

MW01678763

Carla-Krystin Andrad one of those unus people who can take best from different fields and put it all together to create something new and special. A stress specialist with a keen interest in the relationship between the mind and the body, Andrade has used her training as a physical therapist and psychotherapist to develop innovative, practical relaxation and stress/life management programs to help people help themselves.

Why a book specifically on helping *job hunters*? Because in recent years, economic upheaval and dramatic technological changes have affected millions of people around the world. In the past, Andrade provided stress management workshops mainly to corporate clients. Today, she is known for her public awareness campaigns and seminars to help job hunters avoid becoming victims of the job-hunting rat race. Her clients — the men and women who have attended and benefited from these workshops — urged her to write this book because job hunters need all the help and support they can get. And that's exactly what Carla-Krystin Andrade has provided in *Stay in Control.*

STAY IN CONTROL

THE REAL KEY TO JOB-HUNTING SUCCESS

Carla-Krystin Andrade

Trifolium Books Inc.
TORONTO

Stay in Control
The Real Key to Job-hunting Success

Copyright © 1994 by Carla-Krystin Andrade

Copyright under the International Copyright Union. All rights reserved. This book is protected by copyright. No part of it (except the pages so designated) may be reproduced, stored in a retrieval system, or transmitted in any form by any means, electronic, mechanical, photocopying, recording, or otherwise, without written permission from the publisher, or in case of photocopying or other reprographic copying, a licence from CANCOPY (Canadian Reprography Collective), 214 King Street West, Suite 312, Toronto, Ontario, Canada, M5H 3S6.

Care has been taken to trace the ownership of any copyright material contained in this text. The publishers welcome any information that will enable them to rectify, in subsequent editions, any incorrect or omitted reference or credit.

This book is sold with the understanding that neither the author nor the publisher is hereby rendering individual medical nor psychotherapeutic advice. If such advice or other assistance is required, the personal services of an appropriate practitioner should be sought.

All names and identities of individuals have been disguised to protect their anonymity, unless a first and last name are given.

First published in 1994 by
Trifolium Books Inc.
238 Davenport Road
Suite 28
Toronto, Ontario
M5R 1J6
Canada

Canadian Cataloguing in Publication Data

Andrade, Carla-Krystin, 1962-
Stay in control: the real key to job-hunting success

Includes bibliographical references and index.
ISBN 1-895579-30-9

1. Job hunting. I. Title

HF5382.7.A53 1994 650.14 C94-930185-X

Ordering Information
Orders by Canadian trade bookstores, wholesalers, individuals, organizations, and for quantity sales: Please contact Stoddart Publishing Co. Limited, 34 Lesmill Road, Don Mills, Ontario, Canada M3B 2T6; tel. Ontario and Quebec (800) 387-0141, all other provinces (800) 387-0172; fax (416) 445-5967.

Orders for course adoption/educational use: Please contact Trifolium Books Inc., 238 Davenport Road, Suite 28, Toronto, Ontario, Canada M5R 1J6; tel. (416) 925-0765; fax (416) 925-2360.

Design/Illustration: Jack Steiner Graphic Design
Editing/Production: Francine Geraci
Photo of Carla-Krystin Andrade by Headshots

Printed in Canada at Best-Gagné
Printed on acid-free paper.
Last digit is print number: 10 9 8 7 6 5 4 3 2 1

To Len Frenkel, and Nadeige and Chanelle Andrade,
for all their love and support

Praise for the Andrade Method for Job-hunting Success

"After reading Carla-Krystin's book, I now realize that I didn't know how to relax. I was so nervous at interviews I could hardly speak."

—Anna Louise T., laid-off Office Manager, out of work for 8 months, now Administrative Assistant in an international marketing firm.

"Today, there is no such thing as a job for life, so we're all going to have to deal with the stress of job hunting a number of times in our careers. This book tells you what you need to do to keep on top of your life and your job search while you're out there in the trenches. ... Andrade's methods for kick-starting sagging self-confidence and self-esteem should be in every job hunter's arsenal if you want to be competitive in a changing job market."

— John Chrobak, President, Pro Tech Technical Services, specialists in career counseling and placement services for technical and professional personnel.

"Carla-Krystin's workshop gave me the boost I needed to go on. I'm really glad she's written this book for all the people out there who can't hear her in person."

— Frank K., downsized Sales & Marketing Coordinator, out of work 6 months, now working as a Publicity & Promotions Coordinator.

This Book Is for You

Are you a new graduate looking for your first job? Did you lose your job recently, or some months ago? Are you simply looking for a better job? Are you returning to the work force after an extended absence? Whatever your situation, if you are a job hunter, this book is for *you*.

I have worked with job hunters from all walks of life, first as a career counselor, then as a physiotherapist, and most recently as a stress specialist. I have listened to job hunters' stories, shared their pain, and supported them as they sought solutions to the obstacles they faced.

I wrote *Stay in Control* in response to your needs as I have heard and understood them over the years. I have tried to fill this book with answers to the questions most often posed to me by job hunters who telephoned or wrote to me, or who approached me with questions in auditoriums, seminars, workplaces, subway stations, or wherever else we happened to meet. I have tried to make this book practical, down-to-earth, easy to follow, fun and most of all, useful.

Now, it's yours. I hope the information it contains will make your job search more rewarding and bring you lasting satisfaction over the years to come.

—Carla-Krystin Andrade

> Note: *Stay in Control* distills the best of the seminars and programs I offer job hunters into a format that you can use at home. Since I am not able to work with you personally, I recommend that you follow the stress control techniques as you would any other health program—in consultation with a health practitioner.

Acknowledgments

I would like to thank everyone who assisted me on my journey from "a great idea" to the final version of *Stay in Control.* My clients unselfishly shared their stories and their feedback on my work, and inspired my search for new approaches to low-stress job hunting. Trudy Rising, President of Trifolium Books, backed my vision of the book, and Grace Deutsch, Director of Publishing at Trifolium, generously handed out accolades and brickbats throughout its development. Francine Geraci's editorial expertise was essential to the refinement of the manuscript. Jack Steiner gave the finished book its visual appeal.

It was Bill Waddell who got the ball rolling for this project. Len, Chanelle, Nadeige and the rest of my family gave me the support, love, encouragement, and peace and quiet that sustained me throughout production of the various drafts of *Stay in Control.*

CONTENTS

INTRODUCTION

You're Not Alone

"In the last few months I've sent out so many résumés I've lost track of them. And no job yet," confides Lee, an electrical engineer. "The phone isn't ringing. Checking the mail seems pointless. I'm tired of being criticized, judged, and rejected... I'm not sleeping well because of the stress, and I'm suffering for it. I've gotten disorganized. My patience has worn thin along with my confidence. I'm even finding it hard to keep my job search going... My family and friends have stopped asking about my job search. They seem to think it's my fault that I'm not working yet. And sometimes, I find myself agreeing with them."

Does Lee's story sound familiar? If you are now a job hunter, chances are you too have faced the harsh demands of a job search—demands that can take a heavy toll on your self-confidence, personal life, health, and ultimately your chances of finding work.

If you have experienced similar problems, don't blame yourself. You're in good company.

It's Not Your Fault

In recent years, the jobless rate has risen sharply. Not only does it take longer to find a job, but there are fewer jobs available. This is a result of shifts in the world's economic patterns, and the profound technological changes taking place today.

Given such a job climate, you can't afford to get mired in self-blame. You must focus on improving your ability to sell yourself to prospective employers if you want to succeed.

Who's Out of Work?

There is no "typical" job hunter: we vary in age, education, and experience. And now that eight job searches in a lifetime is the norm, we may face a variety of job-search demands at different points in our lives.

People look for work for any of a multitude of possible reasons. Here are some of the most common motives for launching a job search.

Job Loss

"I'd been at the plant for ten years when it closed," recalls Laura, an auto worker. "One day the foreman walked in and told us not to come back to work. I was devastated. I'd worked my way up the ranks and that job meant a lot to me... I've lost a lot and I'm still bitter. I'm also afraid of falling into the same trap again."

Job loss is a major life crisis. Because work plays a central role in our lives, people who lose their jobs (often as a result of downsizing or closures) lose much more than their income. They also lose the structure of their lives, the challenges and rewards associated with work, and the network of people from their field or workplace. Job loss is usually followed by a period of intense emotional upheaval and disorganization as people struggle to come to terms with their losses. Being laid off, or outplaced, can deal such a devastating blow to your self-confidence that job hunting becomes difficult.

Graduation

"'You haven't got enough experience.' If I hear that once more I'll scream," says Trohn, a cosmetology graduate. "How do they expect us to get experience if they won't hire us?"

Recent graduates have just invested time and money in preparing for a new field. Eager to try out their skills, they are usually fresh and enthusiastic about job hunting. Unfortunately, they face two barriers: they lack practical experience, and they enter the work force along with many competitors—their classmates. If there are no jobs available when they graduate, their disillusionment can be severe.

Reentering the Work Force

"Ramona and I are going back to work for different reasons: she's recently widowed, and my kids are finally in school all day. But our fears are the same," observes Sharie. "Here we are, mature women who have run a household for years, yet we're both unsure that we're skilled enough to get a job."

Reentering the work force after any kind of absence carries its own particular stresses. People in this situation often lack confidence in their abilities. At the same time, they may face other problems: the illness or death of a spouse, the need to supplement the family's income, difficulties in arranging child care—all can make the transition back to the work force difficult.

Immigration

"I came to this country filled with dreams and ambition. I want to build a future for myself and my family," says Almaz, a chemist. *"But fulfilling that dream hasn't been easy. In my country, I was highly qualified and had a good job. Here, I'm just another immigrant with no local experience, who doesn't speak the language well."*

Immigrants face the challenge of new opportunity with the hope of success in their chosen country. Unfortunately, their job search is often complicated by language difficulties, adjustment to new customs, lack of local credentials and experience, and the daily demands of trying to rebuild a life in a new environment.

Escaping a Negative Work Situation

"I don't know which is more stressful: being hassled by my boss or trying to land a new job without any of my workmates finding out about it," wonders Junior, a Human Resources Manager. *"Interviewers get suspicious when I don't want to name my boss as a reference. I'm not sure I'll get another job soon, but I know I can't stand another month here."*

People who are trying to leave a bad work situation have an added burden: they may not be able to obtain a reference from their current employer. Throughout their job search, they must deal with the pressure of continuing in an environment that erodes their self-esteem.

These are just a few possible scenarios. Are any similar to yours? Your reason for looking for work will affect the pressures you will face.

Meet the Challenge of Job Hunting

Job hunting can be an exhilarating challenge, an opportunity to shape your future in the way that you want. But it isn't easy.

Your job search probably has not been as straightforward as the ones suggested in some books. Along the way, you may have encountered many problems and frustrations that you didn't expect.

A Roller Coaster Ride

Your job search is probably like a wild roller coaster ride as you adjust to change, juggle your finances, make appointments, deal with hassles, psych yourself up for interviews, and just stay organized—all with no guarantee of result.

The uncertainty of job hunting is often the hardest part to handle. You feel as though you can't get off the roller coaster. Your plans and hopes are on hold, and the threat of a jobless future looms closer each day. The fear can be paralyzing. Yet you cannot postpone the rest of your life while you are job hunting.

Life goes on, and you must continue to participate. Other crises and challenges arise. You still have obligations to the people in your life. It's little wonder that many job hunters find their personal life strained by the pressures of finding a job.

You don't have to buckle under job-hunting stresses and strains if you can anticipate the more common problems.

Anticipate Problems

Job hunters all report facing similar difficulties as their job search progresses:

- Loss of confidence
- Emotional upheaval
- Loss of hope and motivation
- Difficulties with personal relationships
- Recurring health problems
- Poor sleep and low energy levels
- Disorganization
- Inability to manage finances.

Sadly, most job hunters rarely discuss the ups and downs of job hunting with others in the same position. As a result, they don't recognize how common these experiences are. Instead, they believe that they are somehow lacking, and wonder what they did wrong.

You are not a failure if you have experienced any of these difficulties. They are normal reactions to the physically and emotionally demanding process of job hunting. What's important is how you deal with them.

Improve Your Personal Life, Improve Your Job Search

The state of your personal life affects the quality of your job search. It's impossible to maintain an organized, efficient, and thorough job search when you are disorganized, lethargic, emotional, and in ill health. You cannot focus on the mechanics of job hunting—résumé writing, interviewing, networking—and deal with personal or health problems. On the other hand, a personal life that is orderly and satisfying will enhance your job search.

The Andrade Method

Equip yourself with more than the basic job-search skills. Focus on your best resource: *you*. Your self-image, your strengths, your goals, and your determination are the real key to your job-search success.

I have called the approach that I have found most successful for the largest number of people the Andrade Method. The Andrade Method breaks down your job-search strategy into stages and steps that you then rebuild to suit your needs. It shows you how to

- Strengthen your self-image and self-esteem
- Identify your goals and chart ways to achieve them
- Control your stress levels to ensure peak energy and performance
- Reorganize your daily routine for maximum efficiency and enjoyment
- Improve your communication skills and personal relationships
- Make the most of reentering the workforce.

Work through the many practical exercises in this book—Control Builders, Stress Control Plans, Daily Control Plans—to create a job-search program that is personally tailored for *you.*

I have worked with job hunters over the past ten years, first as a career counselor, then as a licensed physical therapist, and later as a specialist in job-search stress. I created the Andrade Method in response to job hunters' needs as I have heard them in my private practice and in public seminars and workshops.

You are not alone in your job search. This book can be your guide. But the rest is up to you. Make this book work for you—and reap the rewards.

STAGE 1

Take Control of Your Job Search

Begin now by taking stock of the effect that your job search has had on your personal life. Then go on to improve your chances for job-hunting success by rebuilding your "core"—your fundamental beliefs about yourself and your abilities. Feeling good about yourself, having realistic goals, and knowing how to withstand criticism will all enhance your job search.

The chapters of Stage 1 will show you

- Where to begin the process of taking control of your job search
- How to create your winning self-image and strengthen your self-esteem
- Strategies for fighting criticism—from within yourself and from others
- Ways of getting your life back on track by setting goals and priorities.

CHAPTER 1

Start Taking Control

Making personal changes is like going on a journey. It's an opportunity to explore, to gather new experiences, and to try doing things differently. At the end of your journey, you may see your life in a new way—and you may have a new job.

Your journey to change begins with four steps:

- Step 1: Decide to Take Control
- Step 2: Plan Your Journey
- Step 3: Get Organized
- Step 4: You're Off!

Step 1: Decide to Take Control

Do you want to take this journey or not? Make your choice. Because if you are to make real changes in your job search and your personal life, your motivation to change must come from within. It's not enough for someone to tell you that you need to change your job-search strategy. You need to say to yourself, "I want to do things differently." You've got to want to change.

Stop and ask yourself whether you are ready to commit to changing some aspects of your job hunt. Don't balk at the thought of making a commitment. A commitment isn't a prison sentence; it's a promise that you make about something that's important to you.

Take the time now to complete Control Builder 1.1: My Commitment to Change. It will help you clarify your personal contract by putting it on paper.

What's In It for Me?

Sometimes people don't feel ready to change unless their situation is dire. Or they'll consider changes only if they can see some concrete gains to be had. If you're not convinced that you need to change, why not check what you might gain from

CONTROL 1.1 BUILDER

My Commitment to Change

Identify why you want to make a change and which aspect(s) of your job search or your personal life you wish to improve. Here's an example; make yours fit your circumstances.

"I realize that my job search is beginning to affect my health. As of today, I promise myself to get more rest and look for other ways to make my job search less stressful."

Date: ____________________

____

____

____

____

CONTROL 1.2 BUILDER

What I'll Gain from Changing

What problems am I currently experiencing in my personal life and job search?	How can I benefit from making a change to address this problem?
Example: I'm irritable/disorganized and I haven't been setting up interviews.	Once I'm calmer/organized I'll be able to send out more résumés and set up interviews.

(Use further sheets of paper as necessary.)

Do the benefits of change outweigh the costs? If you were not able to complete Control Builder 1.1, go back to it now and define (or refine) your commitment to change.

doing so. Work now through Control Builder 1.2: What I'll Gain from Changing, and see if you don't rethink (change!) your views as a result.

Step 2: Plan Your Journey

To get the most out of your journey, you need to identify where you are now, plan your itinerary, and decide where your travels will end. This is a purposeful trip, not one of the rest-and-relaxation variety. Control Builder 1.3: My Personal Plan for Change will guide you.

If your situation seems too overwhelming or too negative to fix, don't try to tackle everything at once. Start small by breaking down *one* problem into specific, manageable tasks. Then take it a step at a time. Set aside a day and time when you will work on this one aspect of change. When you've done this, decide what reward you will give yourself for trying to do things differently.

CONTROL 1.3 BUILDER

My Personal Plan for Change

Check the areas of your life that you wish to change, and note the chapters later in this book that deal with them.

___ Improve my self-image (Chapter 2)

___ Deal with criticism and self-criticism (Chapter 3)

___ Set and achieve realistic goals (Chapters 4 and 13)

___ Get organized; have more productive, rewarding days (Chapters 4, 8-12)

___ Control my stress levels (Chapters 5-7)

___ Learn to relax (Chapter 7)

___ Improve my relationships (Chapter 14)

When I am going to work through this book (specify days and times):

____

____

My rewards for working on these changes:

____

____

People who can give me support in making these changes (specify individuals and the type of support you would like from each):

____

____

____

CONTROL 1.4 BUILDER

My Standards for Success

• What (in one or two sentences) is my life philosophy?

Examples: "Don't burn your bridges behind you." "I believe that you never know when you're going to need someone's help, so I avoid trampling over other people on the road to success."

____

____

____

• How will I know whether my job search has been successful?

Example: "I will have been successful if I can get a job without being overly competitive, manipulative, discourteous, or by discrediting myself in some way."

____

____

____

Choose Your Destination

How will you know when your journey is complete? Many job hunters believe that success is beating the competition to that coveted job, sometimes at any cost. But if success and being a winner just mean getting the job, what does that make you when you don't succeed and beat the rest of the pack? Of course, one of your goals is to get a job. But you can still choose to replace this dehumanizing measure of success with your own, less destructive and more reasonable, standard.

Control Builder 1.4: My Standards for Success gives you the opportunity to formulate *your* standards for job-hunting success.

Step 3: Get Organized

You've planned your journey and decided where it will end. Now it's time to get organized and decide what you want to take with you.

Take a quick look around you. Are you surrounded by clutter? Is your life literally topsy-turvy? Excessive clutter can add to that sense of confusion which already plagues many job hunters. If you're already feeling out of control, then being surrounded by clutter can make you feel even more hopeless.

So clear enough space to be able to sit and compose your thoughts. All you need, in order to work through this book, is a tidy corner, something to sit on, and a couple of pencils.

If you still feel boxed in by clutter, then work outside your home. Take yourself to a quiet spot such as your local library, a friend's house, or a park. Get away from the confusion of your living space. This will help you to focus.

Deal with Mental Clutter

You need an organized frame of mind to get your job search and personal life under control. Because regardless of how tidy you make your workspace, it will be difficult to work towards change if your mind is cluttered. Eventually, you begin to respond to your mental clutter in the same way you'd react to a very untidy room—you avoid going into it. Excessive napping, constant daydreaming, oversleeping, alcohol and drug

QUICK tips

Clutter Control Strategies

TYPE OF CLUTTER	CLUTTER CONTROL STRATEGY
Weighed down by problems?	• Put aside minor problems and concentrate on the important ones. • Clear your mind of problems by writing about them or talking them out to a friend. • Enlist help to carry some of the burden. For example, a credit counseling service can deal with your creditors.
Stressed or depressed?	• Seek professional counseling. • Join a support group. • Begin a physical activity program. • Try the stress-busting tips in Stage 2 (Chapters 5-7).
Too many commitments?	• Put aside 15 minutes daily for quiet time. • Prioritize commitments; eliminate less important ones. • Avoid taking on new responsibilities.

use, and procrastination are some of the different ways in which we avoid facing our mental clutter.

Quick Tips: Clutter Control Strategies will help you get your mental spring cleaning underway.

Take Stock of Your Personal Life

It's possible to make changes in your job search without first taking stock of your current situation. But you run the risk of wasting your time and energy on things that you don't need, such as excess emotional baggage.

"Emotional baggage" is the bundle of hate, regrets, and hangups that we drag around with us from one situation to the next. It weighs you down and stops you from making the best use of your skills.

Don't hang on to your hangups. Try to put aside thoughts about your weaknesses, faults, and previous mistakes. Don't spend too much time with people who don't encourage your efforts to change. Review your Plan for Change and Standards for Success often. Use them to keep yourself on track.

Step 4: You're Off!

Since change is the goal of this journey, why continue to do things as you've always done them in the past? Take a few chances—and see the difference they can make.

Dare to Dream

Have you stopped dreaming about your future? Why? Perhaps you've been preoccupied with the struggle to make it from one day to the next. Or you're too worried about what tomorrow may bring to want to think beyond today. Many job hunters don't dare to dream in fear of having their hopes dashed.

Yet your dreams can give you hope. As you create images of yourself in the future, you fuel your desire to attain your dreams. You'll also stimulate creative ideas about how to achieve them. Imagine yourself in the job you want. Picture what you'll be doing in a few years. Dare to dream.

But be patient with yourself as you learn new approaches to taking control of your job search. Be realistic about the changes that you are trying to make. Focus on what you can change about your role in a given situation, so that you can avoid the pitfall of trying to change other people instead. Remember that there is no ideal way to do things. Don't expect to change your response to job-hunting problems immediately. If you're too focused on seeing immediate results, disappointment may lead you to give up hope.

What's Next?

Now that you have your Personal Plan for Change, Standards for Success, a tidy workspace, and less mental clutter, turn to Chapter 2 to learn how to overhaul your self-esteem.

REMEMBER

- ✔ Your motivation to make changes in your job search and personal life must come from within.
- ✔ Give yourself room to work, deal with mental clutter, and leave your emotional baggage behind.
- ✔ Be patient with yourself as you learn new approaches to taking control of your job search.
- ✔ Dare to dream.

CHAPTER 2

Get Your Self-Esteem into Shape

"I don't even recognize myself these days. Sure, I look the same; but my old personality is gone," sighs Nick. "I cringe at the indignity of being brushed aside by receptionists when I go for interviews. I die inside each time a company says they don't need my services. It's no better at home—my wife is now the breadwinner, and my sons don't treat me with the respect they used to. Every night I lie in bed worrying about the bills and my future. And underneath it all I feel a burning rage. Yesterday, I walked out of an interview wondering where that insecure, stammering idiot that was sitting in my chair came from."

Job hunting is hard on your self-esteem. That's why the Andrade Method starts with your inner core—your fundamental beliefs about yourself and your abilities.

Your Self-Esteem Can Make or Break Your Job Search

Your self-esteem is one of your most important assets as a job hunter. It's hard to find an aspect of your job search that isn't influenced by how you feel about yourself. Your self-esteem affects your

- Goals and standards
- Assertiveness
- Body language
- Negotiating skills
- Persistence in the face of problems
- Performance under pressure
- Satisfaction with your performance
- Optimism about getting a job.

You've got a better chance of getting hired if your self-esteem is high. It's easier to tackle your job search with enthusiasm when you feel confident about your abilities and comfortable with yourself. Prospective employers pick up on your positive attitude.

This is not the case when your self-esteem is low. If you don't believe that you are qualified for, and deserve, a good job, the tone of your cover letters, résumés, phone calls, and interviews is unsure.

Interviews—An Acid Test for Your Self-Esteem

Maria and Ross have similar qualifications and are interviewing for the same job. The difference between them is their self-esteem.

> *Maria, a divorcée returning to the work force, feels comfortable during her interview. She projects confidence in her suitability for the job and readily volunteers information about her abilities. When faced with difficult questions, Maria calmly reminds herself that she can cope with this situation. When asked about her salary expectations, she is prepared: she turns the question back to the interviewer so that she can learn what the company's salary range is. She can negotiate the salary because she knows she's worth it. At the end of the interview, Maria leaves feeling as though she did the best she could and has a good chance at getting the job.*

Ross handles the interview differently.

> *Ross, a recent graduate from a computer training program, is insecure. Having been rejected by several companies, he is no longer convinced that he has anything to offer. He is hesitant and ill at ease during the interview, even though he has done thorough research into the company and its products. His body language reflects his timidity. He sits slumped in the chair with his arms crossed. When questioned, he apologizes for his skills. When given a challenging technical question by the interviewer, Ross panics. He forgets all his research. Then he offers to take a cut in salary if the company will give him the job. Ross spends much of the interview praying for it to be over. He leaves feeling as though the outcome is up to fate and there's nothing more he can do.*

The success of your interview depends on your ability to project a confident and positive image to prospective employers.

"I Can Fake Self-Confidence"

You may think you can fake it, but there is no substitute for genuine self-confidence. False confidence usually doesn't ring true. And it often breaks down into aggressiveness or defensiveness—negative behaviors when you're job hunting. When you know you're faking, you're waiting for the interviewer to call your bluff.

Learning to act confident (regardless of how you feel) can be a good first step in presenting yourself to prospective employers, but ultimately, it's better to have genuine self-confidence.

Your self-confidence is rooted in your self-esteem. When you are job hunting, your self-esteem is constantly under attack. Constantly having to prove yourself to people is unnerving. Even if you usually feel good about yourself, you may begin to wonder, "Is there something wrong with me? Maybe I'm just not good enough."

When you doubt yourself, you feel out of control of your life. And the longer your job search, the harder it becomes to fight off self-doubt. Not having a solid career identity also complicates social interactions and adds to your identity crisis.

"You Are What You Do"

Have you ever noticed how much emphasis some people place on occupations? "And what do you do for a living?" is a question that crops up early in most "getting-to-know-you" conversations. We seem to believe that knowing someone's occupation tells us everything about that person.

To varying degrees, we all buy in to a belief system that says, "You are what you do." As a result, our job becomes a major part of our identity. Many people won't even consider you a competent adult if you don't have a job with a regular wage. Not having an occupation, therefore, is threatening to anyone's self-esteem.

For this reason, job hunters who are not working usually dread the inevitable question, "And what do you do for a living?" They go to great lengths to explain their situation, or continue to identify themselves with their previous occupation: "I'm between jobs." "I'm in advertising." Anything to avoid saying that they are unemployed. Such replies get them off the hook for a while. But dodging the question doesn't ease their shame at not having a job.

Who Do You Think You Are?

It's not just other people's view of you that changes when you're not working. Being unemployed also raises a real personal dilemma. How do you see yourself when the part of your identity that is attached to your occupation is missing? Stripped of the title and benefits of your occupation, you may find yourself wondering who you are.

Control Builder 2.1: Beyond the Looking Glass explores this question.

CONTROL 2.1 BUILDER

Beyond the Looking Glass

- Take a long look in a mirror. What do you see there?

____

____

- Now think about the things that you *can't* see in the mirror. How do you "see" yourself?

____

____

- Put aside your interview spiel for a moment and give a more personal answer to the question: *"Tell me about yourself...."* (Use further sheets of paper if necessary.)

____

____

____

Time to Rebuild Your Core

If your self-esteem has been worn down by job hunting, don't despair. You are about to start building a new, successful job-hunting image.

This process has four steps:

- Step 1: Give Your Core a Checkup
- Step 2: Create Your Winning Image
- Step 3: Try On Your New Image
- Step 4: Strengthen Your Self-Esteem from Within.

Step 1: Give Your Core a Checkup

Checking your self-esteem requires more than a quick look in the mirror. Take a few minutes now to complete Control Builder 2.2: Do You Like What You See? As you work through the exercise, keep the following points in mind.

- Self-esteem is how you feel about yourself, not how others feel about you. You may not like everything about yourself. But there must be some aspects that you feel good about.

CONTROL 2.2 BUILDER

Do You Like What You See?

1. How do you feel about yourself? Check (✔) the answers that apply to you.

Never Sometimes Often

- Do you feel like a fake when people compliment you ?
- Do you have difficulty in personal relationships because you are unsure whether people like you?
- Are you afraid to stick up for yourself because you think you'll be in the wrong?
- Do you dislike your appearance, your voice, your personality?
- Do you constantly compare yourself to others and fall short?
- Are you hesitant to socialize or strike up conversations because you are afraid of rejection?
- Do you find it difficult to do nice things for yourself?

If you answered "often" to more than three of these questions, then your self-esteem needs work. Steps 2 through 4 of this chapter can help you rebuild your self-image.

2. If you had to choose two words to describe the "inner you," what would they be?

sensitive and self-critical

- Your self-esteem can vary. Although you may usually feel good about your skills, you may occasionally feel less secure when in a situation that makes you feel vulnerable.
- Don't confuse self-esteem with success. Being successful doesn't guarantee that you'll like yourself. By the same token, you can still like yourself even if you're not successful by other people's standards.

Step 2: Create Your Winning Image

Revamp your image. Stop explaining your circumstances. When asked what you do for a living, don't refer to yourself as unemployed, outplaced, or laid off. Stop being embarrassed about not working. You *are* working. You are a job hunter—that is your current occupation.

Job hunting is hard work. It takes time and skill. Not only is it demanding, but (as the classified advertisements say) you must be self-motivated; you must take pride in your abilities; you must possess vision, drive, and commitment. You must be a self-starter, looking for a challenge.

In your present occupation as a job hunter, you must value your time and the work that your job search entails. Being a job hunter fills the gap in your identity left by your previous occupation.

Yet there's more to boosting your self-esteem than just identifying yourself as a job hunter. Create a new image for yourself as a basis for your self-esteem. Control Builder 2.3: Profile of the Successful Job Hunter is the starting point for shaping your new winning image.

CONTROL 2.3 BUILDER

Profile of the Successful Job Hunter

(Use further sheets of paper if necessary.)

- What does your job hunter do (in and out of interviews)?

____

- How does your job hunter speak (tone of voice, speed of delivery)?

____

- How does your job hunter dress?

____

- How does he/she treat himself/herself?

____

- What are your job hunter's health habits?

____

- How does he/she treat others?

____

- Does he/she have any other "successful" characteristics?

____

As you work through this exercise, avoid focusing on externals—the stereotypical "look" (tall, perfect body; straight teeth) that is supposed to spell instant success. Think about your ideal job hunter's skills, attitudes, personality traits—let your imagination run free.

In reviewing your list of ideal characteristics, ask yourself the following questions.

- Which of these qualities do you already have?
- Which of these would you like to develop?
- What kind of job hunter would *you* like to be?

Next, work through Control Builder 2.4: My New Job-Hunting Image, using your ideal job hunter as a point of reference. Pick the qualities you think are the most important and that reflect your values.

What do you think of your new image? It's time to try it on.

CONTROL 2.4 BUILDER

My New Job-Hunting Image

Review the Profile of the Successful Job Hunter that you created in Control Builder 2.3. Use it to create your own new job-hunting image.

- Things that I do now that I want to keep as part of my image:

____

____

- Things that I want to add to my image:

____

____

- How I can acquire these skills/traits?

____

____

- When am I going to work on developing these attributes?

____

____

- The first step that I am going to take to become a successful job hunter is to:

____

____

Step 3: Try On Your New Image

Groom yourself to become a successful job hunter and soon you'll begin to feel successful. In real estate, location is said to be the key to success. In job hunting, it's attitude—and yours needs to be the attitude of success.

Begin experimenting with your new image. What ideal attributes have you listed? Are there any skills or habits—such as speaking more clearly, exercising regularly, or eating a healthier diet—that you can begin practicing on a daily basis?

Make success a habit. There are many things you can do to reinforce your new image.

- Surround yourself with people who will support the "new" you
- Read books that reinforce the changes in yourself that you are trying to make
- Join a self-help group that can guide you further in your new direction
- Watch the newspapers for advertisements for free self-improvement seminars. As well, programs on TV or radio are often filled with tips for becoming more successful.

Step 4: Strengthen Your Self-Esteem from Within

A successful outer job-hunting image is merely a starting point to strengthening your inner core. Your challenge now is to make your inner self-image match your new outer image. Your goal is to feel confident and competent, and thereby to become successful in your job search. You can do this by building on your strengths, doing things you enjoy, sticking up for yourself, expressing your feelings effectively, and treating yourself with respect.

Build on Your Strengths

To believe in your new image and feel good about yourself, you need to build on your strengths. After you've been job hunting for awhile, it can be tough to remember what you are good at. We're all good at many things. Take time now to complete Control Builder 2.5: My Strengths, to remind yourself of your skills.

Don't just turn the page on this list of things you're good at. Photocopy it and carry it around with you, or post a copy in a place where you can see it often. Once a week, add to your

CONTROL 2.5 BUILDER

My Strengths

I'm good at many things, such as...

- Job skills:

  analytical, efficient, thorough, speedy, precise, well organized

- People skills:

  polite, assertive, humble, caring, considerate, respectful – christian values

- Communication skills:

  clear, good listener, sensitive & positive but working on vulnerable issues, empathetic. team player

- Other personal characteristics:

  - goal orientated (when given time frame)

list. Every day, take a few moments to remind yourself of your strengths, particularly before interviews. It's a good reminder of all the skills you can point out to prospective employers.

Be Good to Yourself

Do you feel that you don't deserve to give yourself a treat because you're out of work? Or that you can't spend time on leisure activities that you enjoy because you haven't earned your leisure time?

Do the people around you act as though you shouldn't be having fun because you're unemployed? Do your best to ignore them. You deserve to do the things that you enjoy. You're working at landing the job you want, and that's one of the most demanding jobs there is. So if anyone has earned the right to have some fun, it's you.

One of the keys to improving your self-esteem is to be good to yourself. By doing the things you enjoy, you show yourself

CONTROL 2.6 BUILDER

Gifts to Myself

Remind yourself of the things that you enjoy, the things that make you feel good.

- Hobbies that I enjoy:

  - jogging, movies, shopping, reading, volunteering, indoor sports (bowling, pool, work out), video games

- Activities I like to participate in:

  - church, charity runs, special day events,

- Places I like to visit:

  - parks, rec. areas, shopping malls, libraries,

- People I like to be with:

  -

Money is a concern for most job hunters, so try to identify things that are free or inexpensive, such as free concerts, promotional seminars, parades, walks, parks. Be creative and find cheaper ways to do the things that you used to enjoy.

that you value and are willing to take care of yourself. And enjoying your leisure time helps decrease the amount of stress you experience.

So being good to yourself is good for your job search. Rewarding your efforts is a central part of your new job-search strategy. Start now: complete Control Builder 2.6: Gifts to Myself.

(One further note: doing things for yourself is not the *only* way to boost your self-esteem. Volunteer work can have the same effect.)

Stick Up for Yourself

Treat yourself as though you are worth a million dollars, and you will come to believe that you are. And once you do, you're less likely to sit back and allow others to take advantage of you. As you get used to treating yourself well, you will find that you want to stick up for yourself more often.

The price you pay for not sticking up for yourself is high. When you are passive, your self-esteem suffers. You feel that others do not hear you—and in fact, you may not be heard. You end up feeling powerless and angry at yourself and others. You also end up doing things you don't want to do.

Being assertive can help you in your job search. It's a way of communicating to others your belief that you are as valued as they, and are worthy of respect. Assertiveness stems from self-respect and healthy self-esteem. Quick Tips: Eight Points to Assertiveness will help you to keep these principles in mind while job hunting.

As you develop assertiveness, remember that you don't have to stick up for yourself in every situation. You can also choose to keep silent—as long as it is *your* choice.

QUICK tips

Eight Points to Assertiveness

1. When you ask for something, be direct. Don't hedge; state your request clearly.
2. Speak in a clear, firm tone of voice and don't let people interrupt you.
3. Don't make excuses for people who treat you with disrespect. No one has the right to treat you with disrespect.
4. Don't assume that you're always wrong.
5. If you think that you are being treated unfairly, say so.
6. Don't feel that you need to explain or justify yourself every time you say "no."
7. Take responsibility for your own actions. Let other people be responsible for theirs.
8. Feel free to change your mind. Forcing yourself to continue with a plan that you no longer want is self-destructive.

Express Your Feelings

Job hunting isn't just a mechanical task; it is a highly emotional experience. You'll have occasions for pride, excitement, and sheer joy while you are job hunting. You may also have other feelings, not all of them positive. Have you felt any of these emotions during your job search?

- anxiety
- humiliation
- despair
- depression

- bitterness
- self-defeat
- hopelessness
- frustration
- apathy
- resentment
- inadequacy
- anguish
- emptiness

Your emotions have an impact on your job search. At first, the effect may be subtle: defeat begins to show in your eyes, your tone of voice betrays your anger and bitterness, you become defensive during interviews. Gradually, the effects can increase: depression and hopelessness may destroy your motivation, desperation and futility cloud your judgment. You wear your emotions on your sleeve while you're job hunting. And when your emotions are in control, you're not. Don't let your emotions build up and take over.

This doesn't mean that you have to act happy all the time. Repressing your feelings and denying that they exist won't make you feel any better. Nor will alcohol or drugs remove the pain. It's a myth that feelings can be masked or buried; they simply resurface at other times.

To maintain healthy self-esteem, you need to allow yourself to experience the full range of your emotions: acknowledge them, give yourself permission to feel them, and learn to express them *effectively*.

It's important to recognize that you can't "let it all hang out" any time you like. There's nothing to stop you from crying on an interviewer's shoulder, or slamming doors at the unemployment office. But these may not be the most effective ways to express your emotions.

Let Yourself Feel

- Find a quiet and private place. Close your eyes, take a few deep breaths, and allow yourself to feel whatever arises. First, become aware of your bodily sensations. Then, tune in to your emotions.
- Do you ever feel as though you're about to explode? Try releasing some of those feelings by pounding a pillow, working out at the gym, or crying in the shower. But avoid violence to yourself or others—it's not the way to release pent-up feelings.
- There are many possible ways to get in touch with your emotions: talk to a friend, write your feelings down in a journal, talk to the cat—or even yourself.

Don't release your feelings in a way that will cause more harm than good. Match your venting strategy to your situation. Quick Tips: Let Yourself Feel offers some healthy strategies for venting your emotions.

Treat Yourself with Respect

Most of us don't treat ourselves as respectfully as we treat other people. But we should. If you value yourself, then you deserve respect from yourself as well as from others.

Learning to respect yourself is an important part of developing healthy self-esteem. Think about how you treat people for whom you have respect. Probably, you

- Give them your full attention and listen carefully to what they have to say
- Speak politely to them
- Value their time
- Don't make promises to them that you know you cannot keep
- Honor their wishes and requests.

If you treat yourself in the same manner, the people you encounter in your job search will take their cue from how you treat yourself. So show others how you wish to be treated—by treating yourself with respect.

What's Next?

Misguided or misplaced criticism can undermine your efforts to strengthen your self-esteem. Chapter 3 tells you how to take on the critics and win.

REMEMBER

- ✔ Your self-esteem can influence the success of your job search.
- ✔ The many negative aspects of job hunting can erode your self-esteem.
- ✔ It's better to rebuild your self-esteem than to try to fake self-confidence.
- ✔ You can create a successful image for yourself and rebuild your self-esteem by remembering your strengths, doing the things you enjoy, sticking up for yourself more often, expressing your emotions, and treating yourself with respect.

CHAPTER 3

Stand Up to Your Critics

When you are job hunting, it may seem as though the critics are everywhere: people who stereotype and criticize those who are unemployed; interviewers who point out how you don't meet their company's requirements; friends who insist that you're going about your job search in the wrong way; family members who blame you for your inability to find a job. And often, your harshest critic is the one you carry around inside yourself.

Don't take criticism from other people—or yourself—sitting down. Identify the source and how it affects you. Take a stand against your critics, internal or external.

Society Blames Job Hunters

At the root of much of the criticism leveled at job hunters lies a widely accepted belief that unemployed people are to blame for being unemployed. Our work ethic says that if you try hard, you will succeed—so, by the same token, if you haven't succeeded, it must be your fault. As a result, people who have jobs often see those who are unemployed as failures.

Stereotypes of Job Hunters Abound

Stereotypes about the unemployed stem from this animosity and a lack of understanding of the real causes of unemployment. You may have encountered some of the many stereotypes about people who are unemployed: that they are lazy, worthless people who are a burden on society. None of these stereotypes is true. All of them are hurtful.

People use these stereotypes to justify treating job hunters with disrespect. Racist slurs, sexist comments, homophobic remarks, statements that belittle the disabled, sarcastic put-downs—all are disrespectful and unacceptable. So is discourteous behavior, such as an interviewer's keeping you waiting when you have an appointment. Unfortunately, poor treatment of job hunters is becoming commonplace.

Not More Well-Meaning Advice

Along with stereotypes, job hunters often receive unsolicited advice. Advice can be constructive or destructive. Constructive feedback from others, when it is respectfully offered and willingly received, can be helpful to your job search. However, constant criticism from others can crush your pride and your spirit. Buying in to stereotypes does more than hurt your feelings; it can also reinforce destructive self-blame and low self-esteem. Disrespectful behavior can leave you feeling powerless and humiliated. And too much unsolicited advice—even when it's well intended—can leave you doubting your ability.

If the advice you receive seems patronizing or unnecessarily critical, if it's contradictory or confusing, it can be more than just an irritating nuisance. Too much of it can erode your confidence in your own abilities and opinions.

Are You Your Worst Critic?

It's hard not to become critical of yourself after facing stereotypes, disrespectful treatment, and unsolicited advice. And many job hunters become their own worst critic. Even those who begin their job search with optimism and self-respect may come to internalize the criticism and disrespect that others heap upon them. Self-criticism can take many forms, including

- Exaggerating the negative aspects of a situation
- Self-imposed putdowns or devaluing your achievements
- Replaying old criticisms from your past
- Needless worrying.

Self-Blame and Guilt—The Job Hunter's Burden

It's not unusual for job hunters to blame themselves for their circumstances and to feel as though they are getting what they deserve. They assume that they must have done something wrong and are still at fault—otherwise, why haven't they found a job? They end up spending too much time regretting their actions, even if they are not at fault.

We all share society's values to varying degrees. The more we accept these values, the greater the shame and self-blame we may experience when we lose a job or experience difficulty finding one.

Guilt also accompanies job loss and unemployment. The guilt that job hunters feel can become overwhelming when they are unable to meet their obligations, or feel as though they are not pulling their weight. This guilt increases if money difficulties result in financial dependence on others.

Where does the criticism end? Criticism isn't just a personal annoyance. Whether its source is internal or external, it can hamper your job search in many ways.

Self-Criticism Is Costly

> *Mireille is late for her interview. As she rushes into the room she bumps into the coat rack, loses her balance, and falls. "You klutz," she berates herself. "I can't believe you just did that." She notices that the others in the reception area are looking at her. "Great! You've just made a fool of yourself in front of a room full of people," she scolds. Mireille doesn't know where to look or what to do. "You've blown it!" she mutters. Out of the blue, she remembers the teasing she endured as a child: "What a clumsy kid! Let's hope she grows out of it." Mireille flushes; her heart pounds. She wishes that the ground would open up and swallow her. No such luck. Mireille gets to her feet, trying to act nonchalant. "I may as well call it quits," she thinks. "It'll just be downhill from here on."*

Mireille has become a victim of her own self-criticism. Her harsh judgment has destroyed her self-confidence and robbed her of her composure. Given her attitude, her interview will likely be disastrous. Does Mireille's attitude sound familiar?

Don't underestimate the power of putting yourself down. Those self-imposed putdowns aren't harmless. They can cause you to

- Downplay your skills and undervalue your abilities
- Fail to use your skills to their full advantage
- Feel at a disadvantage in difficult situations
- Misinterpret other people's actions
- Fail to choose the course of action that's right for you.

Your self-criticism can also become a self-fulfilling prophesy. For example, if you repeatedly tell yourself that you aren't good enough for the job, your attitude in the interview will signal the same idea to your prospective employer. It won't be surprising if you don't get the job.

Self-blame and guilt eat away at your self-esteem. They punish you and deprive you of the chance to be good to yourself and to enjoy yourself. They also keep you firmly rooted in the past and stop you from making the most of the present. And that can damage your job search by causing you to miss out on opportunities.

So the next time criticism comes your way, don't just accept it in silence. Instead, learn to silence the critics—within you and around you.

Silence the Critic Within

It's difficult to argue convincingly with people who criticize you when you habitually put yourself down. To respond successfully to the critics around you, you must first tackle the critic within.

Self-Talk: Your Inner Critic

We all talk to ourselves. This self-talk is an inner dialogue or running commentary on what is happening to and around us. It's based on all the things that you have heard about yourself, and that you have come to believe about yourself, since you were a child.

Your self-talk is like having your own resident movie critic right inside your head. Whenever you do something, you get a blow-by-blow review based on your interpretation of the situation and your actions. Your self-talk can be negative and destructive, or it can be supportive, empowering, and motivating. Negative self-talk is like a bad movie review—full of scathing remarks. And these negative comments influence how you respond to situations.

Many people don't believe that they engage in self-talk, either negative or positive. They aren't aware of the stream of dialogue inside their heads. Self-talk is a part of you whether you notice it or not. Often, these thoughts arise so quickly that you don't recognize them for what they are. But it is possible to to learn to identify your self-talk.

Get a Handle on Your Self-Talk

To do so, you need to understand how self-talk works. Figure 3.1 (p. 32) shows how self-talk arises in relation to external events, and how you respond as a result.

In Mireille's situation, an event occurred—she fell. Her self-talk about the event was negative: she berated herself, reminded herself of her shortcomings, and told herself that she was unable to cope. She responded by becoming flushed, her heart rate increased, and she felt hopelessly insecure. In the process, her attitude towards her impending interview also became negative.

There is no bigger millstone for a job hunter to carry than

FIGURE 3.1 Charting Self-Talk

Event ⟶ Self-talk ⟶ Response • Mental • Physical • Emotional

What Happened?	**What Did I Say to Myself?**	**How Did I Respond?**
Example: Received a letter turning down my application.	"You've blown it again." "You're never going to get a job. No one wants to hire you."	• Felt really depressed and hopeless about job hunting. • Crawled into bed and slept for the rest of the afternoon.

self-criticism and self-blame. Silencing the critic within you involves four steps:

- Step 1: Track Your Self-Talk
- Step 2: Assess Your Self-Talk
- Step 3: Argue with Your Inner Critic
- Step 4: Keep One Step Ahead of Your Critic.

Step 1: Track Your Self-Talk

Before you can turn the tables on that doleful critic inside your head, you need to know what you're dealing with. Your negative self-talk may not be so obvious as Mireille's. So how do you spot it? Begin with your reaction. That's the easiest indicator.

Each time you find yourself getting stressed, or reacting negatively, stop and check your thoughts. What did you say to yourself just before you reacted? Control Builder 3.1: What Did I Say? will help identify your self-talk.

Whose Voice?

Look closely at what you wrote in the second column of Control Builder 3.1. Do your self-criticisms contain any familiar statements about your shortcomings that have been made by people from your past? Often, we internalize the criticisms of others and repeat them to ourselves without realizing the source of the comments. As a general rule, self-talk statements beginning with "I" reflect your own voice; "you"-statement self-talk often carries messages that have been imposed on you by others.

Once you've identified your self-talk, the next step is to assess it.

Step 2: Assess Your Self-Talk

It's usually easy to distinguish negative self-talk. Does what you are saying to yourself match the facts of the situation? Is your

CONTROL 3.1 BUILDER

What Did I Say?

Have you reacted negatively to a situation recently? Try to recall what you said to yourself and how you responded.

Event ⟶ Self-talk ⟶ Response • Mental • Physical • Emotional

What Happened?	**What Did I Say to Myself?**	**How Did I Respond?**
Example: Fumbled a question about my job history during an interview.	"That does it; now they know what a loser I am."	Felt my face grow hot; didn't hear the next question they asked me.
____________	____________	____________
____________	____________	____________
____________	____________	____________
____________	____________	____________
____________	____________	____________
____________	____________	____________
____________	____________	____________
____________	____________	____________

Make a habit of trying this exercise each time you react negatively in a situation. It will help you to understand your response, and is your first step toward making your self-talk more positive.

interpretation of events realistic? Figure 3.2 (p. 34) lists some common patterns of negative self-talk. If any of these sound familiar, it's time to start talking back to your inner critic.

Step 3: Argue with Your Critic

The next time your built-in critic starts to give you a negative review of something you've done, remind yourself that this is opinion, not fact. Don't just accept this negative assessment. Talk back. Turn the tables and make the review a positive one.

- Review the facts of the situation
- Replace any negative, distorted messages with more realistic interpretations

FIGURE 3.2 Common Self-Talk Traps

TYPE OF TRAP	EXAMPLE
Exaggerating	"I blew that interview. I'll never get another one."
Putting yourself down	"You loser—you never do anything right."
Blaming yourself	"You've blown it! If you hadn't mentioned the layoff, they would have hired you."
Replaying old messages from your past	"You've never been able to make good decisions."
Worrying unnecessarily	"I'm not sure I told them all my skills. They probably didn't like me. I probably won't get the job. How am I going to pay the bills this month?"
Devaluing your achievements	"Oh, getting that interview was a fluke."

- Don't blame yourself unnecessarily
- Try to find something positive in the situation.

Stop Punishing Yourself

Whether or not you believe that you are responsible for your situation, ask whether punishing yourself can help your job search. Even if you have made mistakes in the past—and who hasn't?—continuing to berate and blame yourself does nothing to improve your present situation. It can actually make it worse by paralyzing you, eroding your self-esteem and hampering your job search. Quick Tips: Ending Self-Blame gives you some pointers.

Accentuate the Positive

You may think that when you replace negative self-talk with more positive statements you are lying. You're not. After all, negative self-talk is not necessarily the truth; it is more likely to be inaccurate, or an exaggeration. Positive and realistic interpretations are your goal. In Mireille's case, positive self-talk can turn a potential failure into success.

Mireille is late for her interview. As she rushes into the room, she bumps into the coat rack, loses her balance, and falls. "Oops, I didn't see that coming," she exclaims. "Oh well; these things happen." She looks around and notices that the people in the reception

QUICK tips

Ending Self-Blame

Whenever you feel self-blame creeping back into your life:

- Describe what you now blame yourself for or feel guilty about.
- Explain to yourself what you were trying to achieve when you made those decisions.
- Look at the options that were then available to you.
- Acknowledge that you did the best that you could at the time, given what you knew.
- Forgive yourself for doing the things that you were responsible for; remind yourself of any circumstances that were beyond your control.
- End by giving yourself permission to ditch past blame and guilt.
- For a more active means of purging self-blame, try writing out a list of things for which you blame yourself. Then destroy it.

area are looking at her. "I guess they're concerned that I might have hurt myself," she thinks. She smiles, a little sheepishly, at the others in the room. They smile back. They're nervous too, she realizes. She picks herself up. Not much damage done, but she is flustered. She reminds herself, "Better pull myself together and focus on the interview so that I can be at my best." Mireille takes a deep breath and walks towards the receptionist.

Step 4: Keep One Step Ahead of Your Inner Critic

Get into the habit of feeding yourself affirmations (positive statements) to counteract those habitual negative, self-defeating messages. Control Builder 3.2: Ammunition Against My Inner Critic (p. 36) encourages you to formulate positive statements about yourself.

A Little Flattery Goes a Long Way

It's OK to flatter yourself a little. Say, "I'm going to get a job," "Today I'm going to do well on that interview," or "I've got a lot of skills and experience to offer."

Replacing negative self-talk with more positive statements takes time and practice. Remember, it took time to build up the bad habit of negative self-talk. So give yourself time to break the habit.

Silencing the critic inside you will prepare you for handling the critics around you.

CONTROL 3.2 BUILDER

Ammunition Against My Inner Critic

Review the negative self-talk statements you recorded in column 2 of Control Builder 3.1: What Did I Say? (p. 33). Then make a list of positive statements that you might use to counter this negative self-talk. (Use further sheets of paper as necessary.) Two helpful hints:

- Word your statements in the affirmative. Don't say, "I am not a loser"; say, "I am a winner."
- Frame your statements in the present tense, as though you have achieved your goals. Say, "I am well organized," not "I hope to become well organized."

____

____

Silence External Critics, Too

You don't have to accept other people's verbal potshots—and you shouldn't. Responding to external critics involves three steps:

- Step 1: Expect (and demand) respect
- Step 2: Don't buy in to stereotypes
- Step 3: Disregard unwanted advice.

Step 1: Expect Respect

Self-respect is essential if you want to be a successful job hunter. Don't compromise your self-respect—for example, by assuming a "victim" stance when you telephone a company or walk into an interview, or by accepting poor treatment from those who deal with you.

Prospective employers may have jobs to offer, but they do not have the right to treat you in an offensive or disrespectful manner. You have the right to expect respect from interviewers and other representatives of the organizations where you apply for a job.

This doesn't mean that you have to argue with every disrespectful interviewer whom you encounter. In some cases, you may choose not to address the offense during your interview, but to take appropriate action later. Or you may decide that you simply would not work for a company that treats people badly. Whatever your reasoning, remember—it's your judgment call.

You *do* have options. You don't have to take belittling, racist, sexist, or homophobic remarks from anyone. If an interviewer makes a disrespectful comment to you, you can choose to

- Respond immediately to the remark
- Leave the interview
- Say nothing, but put the remark into perspective for yourself
- File a complaint later with the appropriate authority (Civil Liberties Association or Human Rights Commission, Human Resources department of the company, interviewer's superior, etc.).

Righteous indignation is not the only way to handle such situations. Here's a pithy letter written by Ruth Lyons, who was left waiting in the reception area while her prospective interviewer chatted endlessly on the telephone.

Ruth Lyons
1374 East 54th Street
Belleville

January 26, 199-

Mr. T. Jones
Marketing Director
MPJ Manufacturing
1329 Hyperion Way
Belleville

Dear Mr. Jones:

You asked that I call if I couldn't make my appointment, so that you could put someone else in my time slot. I should have said the same applies to you. You wasted my time. Your behavior is inexcusable.

I waited for you for half an hour. When I left, you were still on the phone. I hate to think how much longer it would have taken you to get around to me.

If I were an important supplier, or a valuable contact, would you have treated me so casually? Probably not. By doing so, you told me that I was less important than your other business contacts. But I don't see myself that way, and that's why I'm sending you a bill for my time.

Sincerely,

Ruth Lyons

Ruth did indeed go on to enclose a bill for her time. How did she feel about sending the letter?

"Of course, I didn't get paid. The man didn't even call to apologize. So what did I accomplish with this acerbic letter? Revenge! I was really mad at this man. By writing that letter, I regained my sense of humor and stopped myself from feeling victimized. So it was worth my time and the postage stamp."

Weigh your options: What action is appropriate to the situation? What action would satisfy you? Do whatever is comfortable for you.

Step 2: Don't Buy in to Stereotypes

Like your own negative self-talk, stereotypes about job hunters are based on opinion, not fact. Treat them just as you would your own self-criticism—argue back!

Don't assume all the blame for not having found a job. Unemployment isn't just the individual's problem; it's part of complex worldwide economic and political conditions. Keep these facts in mind the next time someone throws an unemployment stereotype at you. And don't let stereotypes get under your skin. Try some of the rejoinders listed in Quick Tips: Smashing Stereotypes.

Now you have something to say to people who throw groundless stereotypes at you. But what about people who are constantly hounding you with well-meaning advice?

Step 3: Disregard Unwanted Advice

Constructive criticism can be useful. After all, no one is perfect, and other people can offer valuable insights about our behavior that we may be unable to see. But, in order to be useful, this type of feedback needs to be

- Accurate
- Positive in intent
- Directed at something you can actually change
- Directed at something you are ready to change and want to change.

No matter how well intended the advice may be, you don't have to accept it just because the person has decided to give it. Here are some hints for responding to unsolicited "If I were you..." statements:

- If you think that the advice may be useful and you are open to listening, go ahead and listen. If you want the advice,

QUICK tips

Smashing Stereotypes

STEREOTYPE	RESPONSE
• Being unemployed is just a paid vacation.	Social assistance isn't exactly a paid vacation. I would prefer to have a real salary.
• You get just what you deserve.	I'm not to blame for the economic situation. That didn't happen to punish me for something I may have done in the past.
• People who are unemployed are looking for a free ride.	This is no free ride. For years, I paid taxes and unemployment insurance. I deserve the minimal financial support I'm getting.
• Most unemployed people are shiftless and lazy. They don't really want to work.	The only difference between most people who are working and those who aren't is where the ax fell in the layoffs. People from all walks of life lose their jobs.
• It's your fault if you're unemployed. There must be something wrong with you. Otherwise, you'd have a job like everyone else.	There's nothing wrong with me in particular. There just aren't enough jobs to go around. I've been looking for a long time, and there are few jobs for someone with my qualifications.

note any suggestions that you think may be helpful. And say thank you.

- If the advice is good, but the time and place aren't, then let the advice giver know that you'd be interested in hearing it some other time.
- If you're not interested at all, then by all means tell the advice giver. There are times when one more well-meaning statement can be the straw that breaks the camel's back.

What's Next?

Now that you've got the critics at bay, it's time to move beyond your inner core. Chapter 4 shows you how to begin reorganizing your personal life and job search.

REMEMBER

- ✔ Everyone maintains a stream of inner dialogue, or self-talk, that can be positive or negative.
- ✔ Negative self-talk can take the form of internalized putdowns, messages from the past, or unnecessary self-blame.
- ✔ Negative self-talk, along with criticism from others, can erode your self-esteem, destroy your self-confidence, and hamper your job search.
- ✔ You can stand up to your inner critic by tracking and assessing your self-talk, framing positive rejoinders to habitual self-putdowns, and accentuating the positive aspects of situations.
- ✔ Criticism from others loses its sting if you expect (and demand) respect, don't buy in to stereotypes, and disregard unwanted advice.

CHAPTER 4

Get Your Life and Job Search Back on Track

"I just can't seem to organize my résumés and interviews since I moved in with my sister," says Joel, an environmental technician. "She's been letting me stay rent-free at her place since I graduated, in exchange for help around the house. I thought it would be OK for a few weeks, but I've been here for months now... In many ways, it's a good arrangement: the location is great, and I've got the house to myself in the mornings. But I'm so busy doing errands, and taking care of the house and the kids after school, that I can't seem to pull my job search together. I'm not even sure what I thought I'd achieve by switching careers. I can't tell you how many times I've kicked myself for going back to school. If I hadn't, I'd be in a cozy job right now instead of stuck in this rut."

It's easy to get thrown off track by the changes that come with launching a job search. These changes can shake the very foundation of your personal life and distract you from your job-search goals. When your whole life is in a state of flux, everything feels disorganized, and you may be uncertain of what to do next. Before you know it, you've fallen into a paralyzing rut.

Don't stay stuck in a rut. Far from distracting you from your job-hunting goals, a skillful reexamination of your personal life at this time can actually get your job search back on track.

Job Hunting Means Change

As we saw in Chapter 1, change is an inevitable part of job hunting. Some job hunters initiate their changes willingly: they wish to advance in their field, start a new life in another country, or launch an entirely new career. Others must respond to changes that have been imposed on them, such as being laid off. In either case, embarking on a job search means that every aspect of your life will continue to change—perhaps for some time.

For example, when Joel chose to return to school, he accepted the trade-off of giving up his predictable job and salary in exchange for the challenge and exhilaration of increasing his technological know-how. But when a new job did not materialize immediately after graduation, he was unprepared for the changes that followed: financial dependence on his sister, and a struggle to maintain his original goals in the face of a hectic and unrewarding daily routine. Joel no longer sees himself as an environmental technician with a bright future. It's not that his goals and direction have changed—they've been lost along the way.

"How Can I Have Goals? I Don't Even Have a Job"

Do you, like many job hunters, limit yourself to a single goal—to get a job? Are you afraid to set additional goals for yourself, or to replace the goals you had at the beginning of your job search?

Many job hunters mistakenly believe that goal setting is futile. This is not the case. You can set and achieve goals that are unrelated to whether or not you are working. In fact, *not* setting goals is one of the most detrimental traps you can fall into while job hunting.

No Goals, No Direction

Life without goals is meaningless and directionless. If you don't know where you are headed, you can end up drifting—doing nothing at all. People who have no direction in life tend to be plagued by negative, self-defeating thoughts and self-destructive behaviors.

It's little wonder if your life and job search stall when your original goals are frustrated. But don't stay stuck in that rut. Getting your life and job search back on track involves four steps:

- Step 1: Face the Changes in Your Life
- Step 2: Put the Past Behind You
- Step 3: Balance Your Job Search and Personal Life
- Step 4: Set New Goals.

Step 1: Face the Changes in Your Life

As we discussed in Chapter 1, you can make change work for you. To do so, you must view change as a challenge, not an obstacle. You also need to find something positive in the changes that have occurred in your life.

CONTROL 4.1 BUILDER

Take Stock of Change

Part 1: Taking Stock. Consider the areas listed in column 1, and describe in columns 2 and 3 how these have changed since you embarked on your job search.
Part 2: Finding the Positives. Resist the natural tendency to focus only on the negative aspects of change. For each area, list in column 4 at least one benefit, or one way in which you might turn an apparently negative change to your advantage. (Use further sheets of paper if necessary.)

1. Area	2. Before My Job Search	3. Changes Experienced Now	4. Benefit(s) of These Changes?
Roles/ responsibilities in workplace, community, or family			
Finances			
Daily activities			
Relationships			
Plans/dreams			
Priorities			
Outlook on life			
Other			

Let's begin by looking at what has changed for you since you decided to look for a job. Think back to the time just before you launched your job search and then complete Control Builder 4.1: Take Stock of Change.

If you find it difficult to complete Part 2 of Control Builder 4.1, set it aside until you have finished reading this chapter. Then return to Control Builder 4.1 and see if you are able to fill in column 4.

Now, free yourself to reap the future benefits of change by putting the past behind you.

Step 2: Put the Past Behind You

So there have been changes in your life. Because some changes are more difficult to accept than others, it's common to feel a sense of loss from time to time. But if you often find yourself

- Reliving past decisions you made about your job or career
- Yearning for the "good old days"
- Fearful of moving ahead and making plans for your future

then you are living with one foot in the past. Don't let your longing for what is past stop you from making the most of your future. Start now to put the past firmly behind you.

Acknowledge Your Feelings

Whether you realize it or not, going through the changes you listed in Control Builder 4.1: Take Stock of Change is an emotional experience. As a job hunter, you cannot afford to ignore your emotional responses, because these can influence your job search. They shape your outlook and self-confidence; if unacknowedged or misunderstood, they can add to your uncertainty and hamper your ability to make decisions.

Learn to Let Go

The first step in learning to deal with these emotions is to admit to yourself that you are leaving your old life—or parts of it—behind. Once you let go of the past, you are free to direct your energy into building your future.

Letting go of the past is not easy, especially if your life changes have been imposed upon you. Control Builder 4.2: I Am Standing at a Crossroad can help you acknowledge any "unfinished business" from your past and steer you towards a positive future.

Step 3: Balance Your Job Search and Personal Life

Many job hunters believe that their job search comes before everything else in life—leisure, relationships, household chores, and other personal tasks. Is this your attitude? Do you believe that this intense focus on job hunting will make you more effective and give your job search a competitive edge?

CONTROL 4.2 BUILDER

I Am Standing at a Crossroad

In two or three sentences, respond to each of the following questions. (Use further sheets of paper if necessary.)

1. What will you be leaving behind as you move away from your old life as it was before your job search?

____

____

____

2. What did these things mean to you? How do you feel about leaving them behind?

____

____

____

3. Are there any issues from your old life that you have not yet dealt with—things you wish you had said or done, or any regrets about past actions?

____

____

____

That time is past; you may put these things away now.

4. Remind yourself of the happy memories associated with your old life—things that you can carry with you always.

____

____

____

5. How do you feel about facing your future?

____

____

____

Allow yourself to experience whatever emotions arise—excitement, uncertainty, happiness, sorrow, fear, hopefulness.

☞

6. Next, read through the following passage. Then close your eyes and imagine yourself going through the actions.

Picture yourself standing at a fork in the road. The path behind you represents your old life, with its familiar roles and routines. The paths ahead represent your new future. Be thankful for the knowledge and wisdom that you have gained thus far in your journey. Say goodbye—and move on towards your new life and your new roles. Picture yourself walking forward onto a new path.

People who subscribe to this philosophy often find that their personal life begins to deteriorate after a few weeks of job hunting. And, contrary to expectations, their deteriorating personal life is reflected in their job search: their followup on job leads becomes sloppy, they become disorganized and easily flustered, and their appearance isn't quite up to par.

Make your job search a priority, but don't neglect your personal life in order to do so. A satisfying personal life can enhance your job search by

- Giving you an organized foundation for routine tasks (such as sending out résumés and scheduling interviews)
- Ensuring that your family and friends are there to support and assist you
- Freeing you from distracting emotional baggage.

Both your job search and your personal life deserve "quality time." Let's examine how you can establish and balance goals within each.

QUICK tips

Don't Neglect Your Personal Life

- Put aside a set amount of time each day for personal activities. Your grooming and hygiene, as well as your enjoyment of sports, hobbies, and other leisure activities, are just as important as your job search.
- Don't automatically sacrifice a personal activity when an unexpected job-search task arises. Can you get the task done at another time?
- Make an effort to cultivate and maintain friendships as well as business relationships.
- Set goals for improving the quality of your personal life just as you do for your job search.

Step 4: Set New Goals

When you set goals for yourself, you ensure that you won't just be swept along by the changes you encounter during your job search. Knowing what you are working towards allows you to

- Identify your priorities
- Make sense of new situations
- Stay motivated
- Increase the feeling of control that you have over your life.

Goals ground you in specific, achievable tasks. We all need short-term, as well as long-term, goals.

Long-term goals express your ambitions and aspirations for yourself over several years. Becoming vice-president of corporate sales or buying a house might be long-term goals.

Short-term goals are smaller benchmarks that we can attain en route to achieving our long-term goals. Snagging an interview for the job of district manager of sales or sitting down with a financial counselor to determine what size down payment you'd need for your first home would be short-term goals.

Look Beyond Career Goals

Some job hunters do not set goals for themselves because they are not fully aware of the options available to them. Looking beyond career goals is one way of broadening your horizons. Clarissa, a horticulturist, describes what happened when she sat down to brainstorm the widest variety of goals she could imagine.

> *"I was surprised to see how many different areas of my life I could improve. This is the list I first came up with:*
>
> - *to be more direct in communicating my feelings*
> - *to set a budget and stick to it*
> - *to improve my diet*
> - *to attend a workshop on stress*
> - *to send out thirty résumés this month*
> - *to perfect a good 'sales pitch' to use when I phone companies to inquire about jobs*
> - *to read at least one inspirational book a month*
> - *to spend half an hour per day talking, or writing, to a friend*
> - *to take a night class on art history*
> - *to devote a few hours a week to gardening*
> - *to start playing volleyball again."*

In the end, Clarissa narrowed her list down to the three goals that seemed most important to her at the time: setting a bud-

CONTROL 4.3 BUILDER

Goals I Want to Achieve

Part 1. From the following list, circle three areas in which you haven't yet set long-term goals.

- Personal growth
- Finances
- Physical well-being
- Mental health/emotional well-being
- Spirituality
- Relationships
- Family
- Intellectual pursuits
- Leisure activities
- Job search
- Material possessions

Part 2. For each item circled, specify *one* possible short-term goal that you might set yourself in order to improve this area of your life.

- ____________________
- ____________________
- ____________________

get, sending out her résumés, and making some time each week to enjoy volleyball. These are all short-term goals and relatively easy to achieve. Clarissa reasoned that if she were successful in achieving them over the next month, she could always return to her list and select a further goal for attention.

As Clarissa's list shows, you can set goals within any aspect of your life. Control Builder 4.3: Goals I Want to Achieve can help you brainstorm. By all means, think big when you first draft your list of goals. But be prepared to balance aspiration with reality as you develop the list of goals you'll actually tackle.

Make Your Goals Attainable

Not all of the goals you set can be achieved. Goals that are vaguely worded, or overly ambitious, are doomed to failure as soon as they are conceived. Achievable goals meet the following criteria. They must be

- Concrete, specific
- Within your power to achieve
- Realistic
- Important
- Timely
- Positive
- Gratifying to you.

Let's apply these criteria to Heinz's goals to see how attainable they are.

Heinz is a scientific illustrator whose search for a job has so far gone nowhere. His life seems to have no direction, so he decided to sit down and set some goals. After careful thought he came up with five goals for the rest of the year:

"• *To change how I dress because my brother Gunther says I look like a slob*
• *To stop hating myself*
• *To improve my method of sending out résumés*
• *To make my friend Jesse more sympathetic about my job-search problems*
• *To buy a house*"

These goals are certainly relevant to Heinz, but are they achievable? Let's go through the criteria one at a time.

▪ Concrete, Specific

Attainable goals are worded so that the outcome is specific and clear—in other words, Heinz will know when he has achieved his end. Of all his goals, the one to stop hating himself is the least concrete. How will Heinz know when he likes himself well enough to stop working on this goal?

Of his remaining goals, improving his résumé mailouts and buying a house are the most concrete. Here at least Heinz will easily recognize the end result.

▪ Within Your Power to Achieve

There is no point in setting a goal that is beyond your control or power to achieve. For example, it may be reasonable to try changing your own beliefs and actions, but you cannot control what other people believe or how they behave.

Heinz's frustration with his friend Jesse's attitude toward his job search prompted his goal of reeducating her and making her more sympathetic. While Heinz may be able to tell Jesse about the realities of job hunting, he cannot expect to change her attitude. She will change if—and when—she wants to.

▪ Realistic

A goal may be technically within your power to achieve, yet still not be realistic. For example, it may require more resources (physical, mental, or material) than are available to you now. Or it may be so difficult to attain that it drains all your energy from other goals you might be striving for. The key here is to strike a balance between aspiration—your dreams—and expectation—what you can reasonably seek to achieve given the limits of your situation.

Of all Heinz's goals, his decisions to improve both his style of dress and his method of sending out résumés are the most realistic. He can easily break these goals down into smaller, manageable steps (scanning the newspapers for sales, inviting his brother to accompany him to buy some new clothes; drawing up a mailing list of potential employers; asking Jesse's help in addressing the envelopes). On the other hand, his goal of buying a house is not very realistic, given the current state of his finances.

▪ Important

While it may be realistic to work on several goals at once, you may need to set priorities among them. For example, if two of your goals are to upgrade your home computer system and to get your finances in order, you may need to put the first goal on hold until you've been able to set a budget and stick to it long enough to save some money. There may or may not be a logical order to your goals; it's up to you to identify your priorities.

In Heinz's case, his job search has stalled mainly because of his erratic manner of sending out résumés. In the short term, his number one priority should be to improve his mailing system. Once his résumés have been properly prepared and mailed, he might consider taking an afternoon off to get his wardrobe into shape.

Return to Part 2 of Control Builder 4.3: Goals I Want to Achieve (p. 48) and number your goals in order of priority.

▪ Timely

Timing is key. In working toward your goals, you need to pay attention to logical priorities, deadlines, and windows of opportunity that may not always be there.

Yet timeliness also means being flexible enough to reorganize your priorities in response to changing circumstances. For example, if just the computer you need becomes available at a bargain price, and your uncle offers to lend you the money on terms of repayment that you can manage, then you may be able to achieve the goal of upgrading your computer system without sacrificing the goal of straightening out your finances.

For Heinz, organizing his résumé mailouts is his most timely goal. While buying a house is not an attainable goal given the one-year time frame he has set for himself, it might become an attainable *long-term* goal if his career prospects improve over the next year.

▪ Positive

Goals that are worded positively are the most motivating to work on. For example, "I will stop skipping meals and eating junk food" is a valid goal, but a better one might be, "I will sit down to three regular, balanced meals per day." Not only is there a recognizable outcome; the wording itself boosts your self-esteem.

Henz's goal "to stop hating myself" is not only vague, it is negative in focus. A more positive reframing might be, "Once each day I will reflect on all the qualities I like in myself."

Phrase your goals in the positive rather than the negative. There is more incentive to work on a goal that promises improvement and heightened self-esteem than one that emphasizes failure and self-blame.

▪ Gratifying to You

For a goal to be attainable, you have to want it; it must gratify you. If you agree to follow someone else's agenda, then you must find something in it for yourself.

In Heinz's case, he won't be motivated to change his style of dress if he doesn't share his brother's opinion that he is poorly groomed. If he disagrees with his brother's judgment, he would be better off omitting this goal.

You now have seven criteria to guide you in distinguishing between achievable goals and those that are likely to be doomed to failure. Control Builder 4.4 will help you evaluate the personal goals you identified earlier in this chapter.

CONTROL 4.4 BUILDER

How Achievable Are My Goals?

Review your goals from Part 2 of Control Builder 4.3: Goals I Want to Achieve (p. 48) and list them below. Then score each goal according to the seven criteria shown in the right-hand column. (Use further sheets of paper if necessary.)

Goal | **Score**

- ____________________

Concrete: ______
In my power: ______
Realistic: ______
Timely: ______
Important: ______
Positive: ______
Gratifying: ______

Total: ______

- ____________________

Concrete: ______
In my power: ______
Realistic: ______
Timely: ______
Important: ______
Positive: ______
Gratifying: ______

Total: ______

- ____________________

Concrete: ______
In my power: ______
Realistic: ______
Timely: ______
Important: ______
Positive: ______
Gratifying: ______

Total: ______

Score your goals as follows:

- Concrete: 2 points
- Within my power to achieve: 2 points
- Realistic: 2 points
- Timely: 1 point
- Important: 1 point
- Positive: 1 point
- Gratifying to me: 1 point

If any one of your goals totals less than 6 out of 10 points, revise it or substitute another that meets these criteria.

QUICK tips

My Mini-Goal for Today Is...

My mini-goal for today is to (choose one)

- Send out five résumés after breakfast
- Get out of the house
- Wash, wax, and polish the car
- Call three potential job contacts
- Bring my checkbook and household bills up to date
- Prepare a beautiful, nourishing meal and eat it slowly
- Practice the guitar for half an hour
- Pick up a course catalogue
- Do twenty minutes of T'ai Chi
- Phone a friend
- Repair the bathroom faucet
- Give the dog a bath
- Other: ____________

A Goal a Day Keeps Negative Thoughts at Bay

If your personal life and job search have settled into such a rut that you're feeling too low on energy even to contemplate the future, give yourself a kick-start by setting one easy, short-term goal each day. Even a mini-goal that you can achieve quickly is a great ego booster, because it gives you an immediate sense of accomplishment.

Some of the shorter-term goals you set for yourself in Control Builder 4.3: Goals I Want to Achieve (p. 48) may be suitable one-day mini-goals; or try some of the suggestions in Quick Tips: My Mini-Goal for Today Is... You can choose a different mini-goal each day to suit the demands of your schedule, or simply your inclination for that day.

Keep Your Goals in Perspective

Goals are not necessarily ends in themselves. Rather, they are signposts that show you what you may accomplish and where you are headed. They are meant to help, not enslave you. Keep them in perspective. And be prepared to modify or discard goals that no longer fit.

What's Next?

With your goals in place, you have completed Stage 1 of getting your personal life and job search back on track. Now move on to Stage 2 to learn how to bring your stress levels under control.

REMEMBER

- ✔ A well-organized personal life can enhance your job search. Don't give your job-hunting tasks top priority at the expense of your personal life.
- ✔ Let go of the past so that you can carry out your job search effectively and make the most of your future.
- ✔ Set a variety of life-enriching goals that you can achieve whether you have a job or not. They will provide direction and meaning for your personal life and your job search.

STAGE 2

Control Your Stress Levels

You have begun the process of building your job-hunting success by strengthening your core. So far you have

- Increased your understanding of your experience of job hunting
- Given your self-esteem a boost
- Learned techniques for countering criticism
- Set some realistic goals.

Now you are ready to move beyond your core to take control of your stress levels.

Chronic stress is one of the greatest enemies you'll encounter during your job search. The chapters in Stage 2 will give you the tools you need to reduce and prevent chronic stress.

You will learn

- The facts about chronic stress: how it affects you physically and mentally
- A way of understanding stress that gives you control over your stress levels
- Stress control strategies that you can use
- A method for creating your own Stress Control Plan
- Step-by-step guidelines for beginning a home relaxation program.

CHAPTER 5

Chronic Stress: A Job Hunter's Worst Enemy

"I didn't understand what was happening to me," recalls Josie, a paralegal assistant. "After a month of job hunting, my headaches were more frequent and I was having trouble getting to sleep at night. Then there was the irritability and forgetfulness. I was falling apart, and so was my job search. Then I started having anxiety attacks—sweating and heart pounding before interviews. I knew then that I had to talk to someone. I was surprised and relieved when the counselor suggested that my problems were stress related. I'd always associated stress with having a hectic job—I never thought I could be under stress when I wasn't working."

At this very moment, chronic stress could be hampering your job search. And you may not even realize this is happening.

Chronic stress occurs when your stress levels are too high, or when stress lasts for prolonged periods. Chronic stress is destructive. It exhausts you and leads to stress-related physical, mental, and behavioral problems.

Stress-related problems can hamper your job search and diminish the quality of your personal life. The longer your job search goes on, and the more competitive the job market, the more likely you are to experience chronic stress.

Fortunately, you can reverse most symptoms of chronic stress by using proven stress control techniques. You can even prevent chronic stress from occurring.

Begin taking control of your stress levels now. This chapter explores how the stress cycle works. You'll also learn to recognize the difference between "good" stress and chronic stress, and how each affects you.

Stress Is...

A surprising number of myths and misconceptions about stress persist.

More Than an Event

Some people think that stress is an event, something that just happens to them. They believe that the amount of stress they experience depends on the number of crises they've been through in the past year. But there's more to stress than external events.

Perhaps you know someone who has been through many crises, yet who has not succumbed to chronic stress. By the same token, there are many people who suffer from stress-related problems, yet have few crises in their lives. Clearly, events don't automatically result in stress.

More Than Just a Physical Response

Others associate stress with their physical, behavioral, and emotional response to situations. Yet two people facing the same crisis can respond differently—one can become stressed while the other remains calm. So there must be more to stress than an automatic physiological response.

More Than Your Personality Type

Another popular view is that your personality influences the amount of stress you experience. Researchers have identified various personality traits and styles that they consider to be more stress prone or stress resistant. Yet people who have the same personality type can still respond differently to stressors. Your personality alone is not enough to predict how much stress you experience.

Stress Involves Your Thoughts

Psychologist Richard Lazarus changed the way in which we understand stress by pointing out that thoughts are an important part of the stress cycle. We all interpret situations based on our previous experience and knowledge. This is why different people can react differently to the same stressors.

The Stress Cycle

The stress cycle shown in Figure 5.1 (p. 58) is similar to the process discussed in Chapter 3.

First of all, a stress-provoking event occurs. Such events can include crises, losses, changes (either positive or negative), or simply the hassles of everyday life and job hunting. Then, your self-talk kicks in. You assess the event mentally

FIGURE 5.1 The Stress Cycle

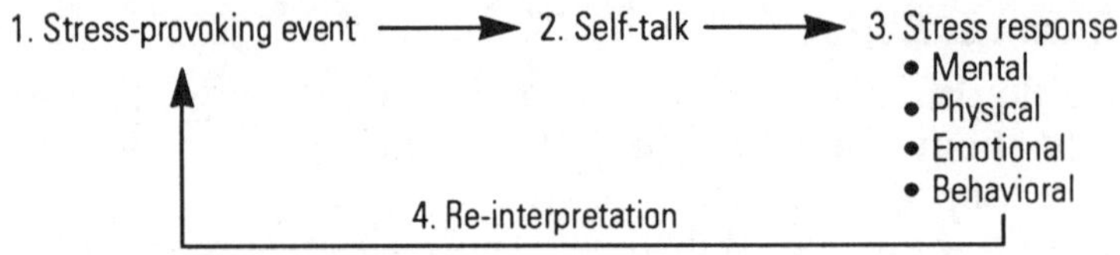

and decide whether it poses a threat to you, and whether you have sufficient resources to cope with the demands of the situation. This is the point at which you decide whether the situation is stressful for you. Your decision will either trigger the stress response, or eliminate the need for it. Finally, the stress response occurs, and your physical and mental function, emotions, and behaviors change as a result. For example, your breathing may become faster, your palms may sweat, you may feel agitated or panicky.

Since this is a cycle, it follows a predictable course. That means you can short-circuit the stress response by reappraising the situation. For example, as the event unfolds, you may become aware of fresh aspects to the situation, or may act in a way that changes your evaluation of the threat and your ability to cope. Based on your new perspective, you may change your approach, or decide that the situation is not stressful after all.

Self-Talk: The Heart of the Stress Cycle

The driving force throughout this process is your self-talk. This doesn't mean that your stress is "all in your head" or imaginary. It means that a situation isn't stressful until you think it is. Your self-talk is what determines how much stress you experience in a given situation.

But what about life-threatening situations? Aren't these automatically stressful? Not necessarily. Many people who often face high-risk situations, such as stunt actors, emergency rescuers, or hobbyists such as sky divers and mountaineers, have trained themselves to eliminate or reduce the amount of stress they experience. They are able to do so by controlling their self-talk. When a stress-provoking event occurs, they choose not to interpret it as being stressful.

The Stress Response

The stress response is based on a primitive reaction called the fight-or-flight response, as identified by the physiologist Walter Cannon. This response prepares the mind and body for self-defense—that is, either to fight, or to get out of the situation. It involves a complex chain of physiological reactions:

- The sympathetic nervous system is stimulated
- The body releases adrenalin, cortisone, thyroid hormones, and endorphins into the blood stream in order to protect the body and speed up the metabolism
- Both heart rate and respiration become faster so that more blood and oxygen can be pumped through the system
- The blood thickens; fuel (in the form of cholesterol and blood sugar) is secreted
- All senses become more acute
- Some systems, like the digestive system, slow down because their function during an emergency is less important.

Some people believe that the fight-or-flight response is the source of our problems with stress. Originally an adaptive behavior that evolved to protect early humans in life-threatening situations, the fight-or-flight response has in many ways become the bane of our existence.

Why? Because we use it in situations for which it was not intended. Not all stress-provoking situations are life-threatening, but the body doesn't know that. As a result, we use the fight-or-flight response more frequently than our bodies were designed to withstand.

Also, we prolong the response. The fight-or-flight response is an immediate, short-term mechanism, intended to last only until the dangerous situation is resolved. The body is then supposed to return to its resting state. Often, this is not the case, as our stress-provoking thoughts keep our bodies in a state of emergency long beyond the need.

Too Much Wear and Tear

Our bodies were not constructed to withstand the demands of the fight-or-flight response for long periods. Hence, problems occur when we experience high levels of stress over time.

The fight-or-flight response affects all your organ systems: respiratory, nervous, circulatory, digestive, urinary, musculoskeletal, endocrine, reproductive, integumentary, and immune. As these systems fatigue, you gradually develop a range of physical and mental health problems. Figure 5.2 lists some of the signs of chronic stress.

Imagine how these physical, psychological, and behavioral signs of chronic stress can affect your ability to carry out your job search.

Chronic Stress Sneaks Up on You

Chronic stress catches most job hunters off guard, partly because the signs and symptoms develop gradually. People who are busy

FIGURE 5.2 Signs of Chronic Stress

Behavioral	Physical	Mental/Emotional
• Defensiveness • Poor decision making • Loss of temper • Disorganization • Withdrawal • Sleeping more/less • Increased use of drugs, alcohol, tobacco • Impaired social relationships	• Sweating • Muscle tension • Heart pounding • Stomach problems • Headaches • Altered sleep patterns • Restlessness • Fatigue • Change in sex drive (increase or decrease) • Frequent illness	• Forgetfulness • Poor concentration • Racing thoughts • Anxiety • Hopelessness • Insecurity • Anger • Depression

with job-search tasks may fail to notice gradual changes in their physical and mental health and behavior. They think that what they are experiencing is simply part of job hunting.

Others (especially those who have many unfilled hours) don't expect to have any stress at all, simply because they have few commitments. But this can be as stressful as having too many.

Job hunters also need to be able to distinguish between chronic stress and "good" stress.

Stress Isn't All Bad

Not all stress is bad for you; a little can be beneficial. We all need *some* stress in our lives. Lack of challenge, stimulation, and excitement can be as negative as having too much stress. Life would be unbearably stagnant without novelty and excitement.

Challenge, excitement, and change enrich our lives. And the benefits of "good" stress are as numerous as the negative effects of chronic stress.

In moderate amounts, stress can

- Increase your productivity
- Enhance your creativity
- Motivate you
- Instill a sense of purpose and reward
- Sharpen your thinking and lead you to deeper insights
- Energize you
- Improve your performance
- Heighten your senses
- Help you to push yourself beyond your usual limits.

Your next task, then, is to distinguish between the levels of "good" stress that energize you, and the levels of chronic stress that sap your energy and create problems in your job search and personal life.

Job Hunting Is Stressful

As a job hunter, you face many stress-provoking situations. High unemployment, a highly competitive job market, strained finances, and changes in your personal relationships—all can add to your feelings of uncertainty and loss of control.

Your personal stressors (stress-provoking situations), and how you experience them, will be unique to you. Control Builder 5.1 (p. 62) will help you identify your own worst stressors. Then you will devise a Stress Control Plan to deal with them.

Bear in mind that there is more to stress than the events you experience. Your interpretation of these situations is also important.

Chart Your Stress Profile

Control Builder 5.1: My Worst Stressors is your first step to identifying the sources of your personal stress. It's important to know how much stress you have. But no single quiz can ever give you an accurate indication of your stress levels, because no checklist can ever be all-inclusive.

The symptoms of stress are many and varied: from restlessness, insomnia, anxiety, and racing thoughts at one end of the spectrum to withdrawal, lethargy, excessive sleep, and depression at the other. You have your own combination of physical, psychological, and behavioral responses to stress. As you go through this chapter, focus on how stress affects *you*. To do this, you are going to chart your personal Stress Profile. This will be one of your most important tools for controlling your stress levels during your job search because your Stress Profile

- Defines your unique signs of stress and charts exactly how your stress levels are affecting you
- Can help you identify the situations you find most stressful
- Signals when you begin to cross the line from "good" stress and enter the chronic stress zone
- Is your cue for when you need to use a stress control strategy.

Control Builder 5.2: My Stress Profile (p. 63)may take as long as a week for you to complete, but it's well worth the investment of time to learn just how *you* respond to stress-provoking situations.

CONTROL 5.1 BUILDER

My Worst Stressors

Part 1. Use the categories in the left-hand column to identify your specific personal stressors in the middle column. (Use further sheets of paper if necessary.)
Part 2. After you have completed the middle column, take a moment to rank (assign a priority to) each of your stressors, beginning with #1 = your worst stressor.

Area	Specific Stressors	Ranking
Personal issues?	• •	______
Job search?	• •	______
Family?	• •	______
Finances?	• •	______
Health?	• •	______
Red tape?	• •	______
Other sources of stress?	• •	______

Don't Be Alarmed!

Yes, this is *your* stress profile. But don't be alarmed by the number or type of symptoms that you've listed. *Most symptoms of chronic stress are reversible. And you can also prevent these and other symptoms from occurring.*

This stress profile is an important tool for controlling your stress levels. Here's how you can use it every day to monitor and identify your response to stressors.

Once you've charted your profile, begin to watch for these telltale signs. Take note of that familiar headache that begins behind your eye, the tightness that knots your stomach, or the sudden swamping feeling of insecurity. Quick Tips: My Stress

CONTROL 5.2 BUILDER

My Stress Profile

Over a period of several days to a week, observe your reactions to everyday situations (not just those directly related to your job search). Using the questions below to guide you, list your observations in the appropriate columns.

1. Behavioral	2. Physical	3. Mental/Emotional
________________	________________	________________
________________	________________	________________
________________	________________	________________
________________	________________	________________
________________	________________	________________
________________	________________	________________
________________	________________	________________
________________	________________	________________
________________	________________	________________

Column 1: Behavioral. Begin by noting any changes in your behavior—these are often the easiest signs of chronic stress to spot. What do you do when you get stressed out? Withdraw? Sleep more or less? Eat more or less? Lose your temper? Cry? Make excuses? Get disorganized? Drink? Pace?

Column 2: Physical. As your behavior changes, note what happens to your body. What physical signs of stress do you experience? Butterflies in your stomach? Headaches? Loss of appetite? Heart pounding? Rapid, shallow breathing? Dry mouth? Tense muscles? Restlessness or fatigue?

Column 3: Mental/Emotional. Finally, note your psychological signs of stress. Chart the changes in your mental function, such as racing thoughts, forgetfulness, confusion, poor concentration. What emotions do you experience? Depression? Anger? Anxiety? Frustration? Hopelessness?

Barometer (p. 64) gives you a practical spot-check for assessing your stress levels throughout the day.

When you notice *your* signs of chronic stress, that is a signal that you need to get your stress levels under control. Chapter 6: Build Your Own Stress Control Plan discusses a variety of techniques for managing the stresses in your life.

QUICK tips

My Stress Barometer

The Stress Profile you created in Control Builder 5.2 (p. 63) can serve as a barometer to tell you quickly how much pressure you're under.

- **High Pressure/Really Stressed**
  Feeling out of control; experiencing more than 5 symptoms of chronic stress from your Stress Profile.
- **Medium Pressure/Somewhat Stressed**
  Aware of strain; experiencing 2-5 symptoms of chronic stress from your Stress Profile.
- **Low Pressure/Hardly Stressed**
  Generally relaxed; rarely notice any signs of chronic stress from your Stress Profile.

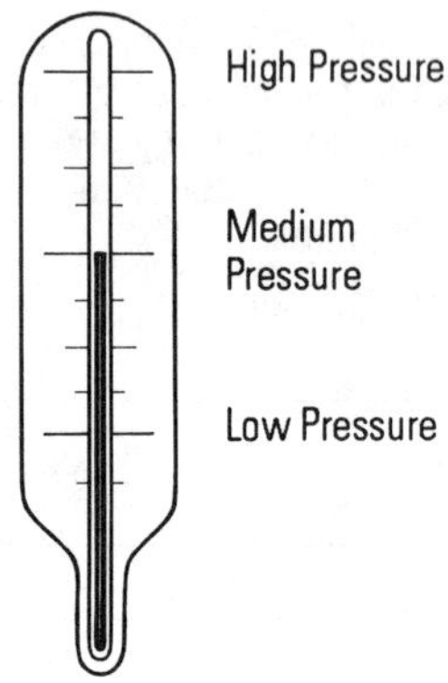

Costs Versus Benefits

Remember, some stress can be good for you and your job search. For example, getting psyched up for an interview—being excited and "on your toes"—can give you just the edge you need to sharpen your performance.

Don't fear stress or attempt to eliminate it from your job search. Strive to keep your stress levels under control so that you can reap the benefits of "good" stress without paying the

CONTROL 5.3 BUILDER

Do My Stress Costs Outweigh My Stress Benefits?

Like everything in life, stress has its pros and cons. Are you balancing the costs and benefits of stress? (Use further sheets of paper if necessary.)

Positive Effects of Stress on My Job Search	Negative Effects

price of chronic stress-related problems. Control Builder 5.3 weighs the costs of stress against the benefits.

Balance "Good" and Chronic Stress

If you have listed more costs than benefits in Control Builder 5.3, don't despair. Your challenge while you are job hunting is to get into the "good" stress zone by balancing the costs and benefits of stress. And you've already taken some important first steps towards doing so. As a result, you are well on the way to taking control of your stess levels.

What's Next?

It's time to take concrete action to control your stress levels. The next two chapters will show you how to use the principles of stress control to balance your stress levels and overcome chronic stress.

REMEMBER

- ✔ Your self-talk plays a major role in how you experience stress. Negative self-talk increases the amount of stress you experience.
- ✔ Some stress can be good for you. However, chronic stress is not. Chronic stress can cause physical and mental health problems and changes in your behavior that can hamper your job search.
- ✔ Many job hunters fail to recognize their early warning signs of chronic stress.
- ✔ Most symptoms of chronic stress can be reversed. Stress control techniques can also prevent chronic stress and its consequences.

CHAPTER 6

Build Your Own Stress Control Plan

Control (vt): to exercise restraining or directing influence over: regulate, curb. . . : to have power over: rule . . . : to reduce the incidence or severity of esp. to innocuous levels. . . . (Webster's Third New International Dictionary)

You know now that stress is not something that just happens to you, and that your thoughts and decisions play a role in how you experience stress. Thus, stress control is active, not passive. It requires that you acknowledge the effects of your appraisals and self-talk, and consciously change your behavior.

There are several possible ways to control your reactions. For example, you can choose to

- Cope with crises that arise
- Identify and change your negative self-talk
- Short-circuit the fight-or-flight response.

You may not be able to prevent crises or hassles, and you don't have to change your personality. But you *can* use your thoughts to control your stress levels.

Don't sit back and wait for chronic stress to ruin your job search when there are proven techniques to keep it in check. Learn the Five W's of stress control. Then, create and apply your own Stress Control Plan.

The Five W's of Stress Control

Who?

You.

You are the person best equipped to change your stress levels. You know how your body feels, which emotions you experience, and how you think as you face stressful job-search situations.

If the stress of your job search seems overwhelming, you may not feel as though you can change what you are experiencing. But it *is* possible to control your levels of stress, regardless of what is currently happening in your life.

What?

In practical terms, stress control involves breaking the stress cycle that we examined in Chapter 5 (Figure 5.1, p. 58). Because this cycle has four distinct stages—event, self-talk, response, and re-interpretation—there are four points at which you can break it.

- **Change the event.** Anticipate and reduce job-search stress, such as that associated with interviews, telephone calls, rejection letters, etc.
- **Think low-stress thoughts.** Negative self-talk is the driving force of the stress cycle. Review the techniques you developed in Control Builder 3.2: Ammunition Against My Inner Critic (p. 36) and use these to break your stress cycle.
- **Don't panic.** Pounding heart, racing thoughts, and other physical and mental responses are not inevitable reactions to stress. You can learn to interrupt and even control these unpleasant symptoms.
- **Think it over.** Even if your initial reaction is negative, you still get a chance to regain control by rethinking the situation. Job-search crises, such as being late for an interview or not mailing your résumé on time, are rarely as bad as they first seem.

When?

It's never too late, or too early, to control your stress levels. There's more to controlling stress than just staying calm. You can—and should—apply stress control techniques before, during, and after any stress-provoking situation to

- Prevent stress
- Stay calm during the situation
- Unwind when the crisis is past.

Where?

Anywhere and everywhere.

Stress control isn't limited to the place where you experience your stress, because it begins where your stress begins—in your mind. There are many stress control strategies that you can do just about anywhere.

Why?

To stay in the "good" stress zone.

Too much or too little stress can adversely affect your health and your job-search performance. The goal of stress control is to have some challenge in your life while keeping your stress levels from accumulating and becoming destructive.

There are no magic numbers that dictate how much stress is acceptable to you. It is up to you to learn how *you* react to stress and what your levels of tolerance are.

Creating a Stress Control Plan

You are unique. Your stress is not like anyone else's, so don't expect a "one size fits all" approach to controlling it. The Andrade Method encourages you to build your own personalized Stress Control Plan to fit your needs, your resources, and your stressors.

Developing your Stress Control Plan involves ten steps:

- Step 1: Identify Your Stressor
- Step 2: Note Your Reactions
- Step 3: Spot Your Negative Self-Talk
- Step 4: Cultivate Positive Self-Talk
- Step 5: Choose Your Strategies
- Step 6: Evaluate Your Strategies
- Step 7: Find Support for Your Plan
- Step 8: Test Your Plan
- Step 9: Refine Your Plan
- Step 10: Write a Reminder

This chapter guides you through each step. You'll finish by filling in your personalized Stress Control Plan Worksheet. A full-size, blank version of this worksheet (which you may photocopy) appears on pages 80-81.

To begin, let's see how Roxanne, who recently completed a fire fighter training course, filled in her Stress Control Plan Worksheet (Fig. 6.1).

Step 1: Identify Your Stressor

Roxanne is now looking for her first job. Although she performed well during her training, she panics during interviews, which unnerve her so much that she is often unable to sleep the night before.

In filling in Step 1 on her Stress Control Plan Worksheet, Roxanne readily identified interviews as her chief stressor. But this quick diagnosis alone would not be enough to help lower her stress levels and improve her performance.

FIGURE 6.1
Roxanne's Stress Control Plan Worksheet

Step 1: **Identify my stressor**	The situation I find stressful:	*Interviews, especially those with timed tests.*
Step 2: **Note my reaction**	My response/cues that I'm stressed:	*My heart pounds, my thoughts race, my hands shake, my mind goes blank.*
Step 3: **Spot negative self-talk**	My negative self-talk in this situation:	*I'm not ready; I always make stupid mistakes; I run out of time; I never do well on timed tests.*
Step 4: **Cultivate positive self-talk**	Positive statements I can use in this situation:	*I'm OK; I am calm; I know the material I'm being tested on.*
Step 5: **Select my strategies**	Before:	*Ask whether interview involves a timed test; practice; take a tranquilizer; be well rested.*
	During:	*Positive thoughts; pleasant imagery; set an alarm; chant; deep breathing; read test through.*
	After:	*Go for a walk; congratulate myself; glass of wine; nap.*
Step 6: **Evaluate my strategies**	Before:	*Practice with a timer; be well rested.*
	During:	*Positive self-talk; pleasant imagery; deep breathing; alarm; read test through.*
	After:	*Go for a walk; congratulate myself; nap.*
Step 7: **Find support for my plan**	Type of support I would like; people/agencies who can support me:	*Practice tests at Job Club; call Jean for pep talk.*
Step 8: **Test my plan**	Before:	*Set alarm, positive self-talk, read test through — OK; keep.*
	During:	*Imagery — too much time, distracting; don't keep.*
	After:	*Deep breathing — OK, but hard; keep (and practice)*
Step 9: **My improved plan**	Before:	*Positive self-talk; deep breathing; practice tests; be well rested.*
	During:	*Set alarm; read through exam; deep breathing.*
	After:	*Go for a walk; congratulate myself; phone Jean.*
Step 10: **My reminder to myself**	Date:	*April 1 Went to Job Club for practice tests...* *April 6 Took a real timed test; did deep breathing...*

What's the Real Problem?

Stress control strategies are most effective when they match the source of stress. Roxanne needed to identify the specific pressures during an interview that cause her to feel stressed. On reflection, she ruled out shyness: an outgoing woman, she had no difficulty establishing a rapport with her interviewers.

However, her self-confidence crumbled whenever she was required to complete a timed, written examination. This situation always reminded her of her poor performance on exams throughout high school. In her resulting panic, she often missed even easy questions for which she was well prepared.

Once she identified the real problem behind her stress, Roxanne was able to explore her responses.

Step 2: Note Your Reactions

Each of us has certain cues that tell us we are becoming stressed. In Roxanne's case, she identified four:

"Whenever I take a timed test,
- *My heart pounds*
- *My thoughts race*
- *My hands shake*
- *My mind goes blank."*

Roxanne's signs and symptoms of stress were easily recognizable. This made it possible for her to monitor her self-talk. Negative self-talk is itself a powerful stressor, and can trigger the stress response.

Step 3: Spot Your Negative Self-Talk

Roxanne wrote out her negative self-talk on her Stress Control Plan Worksheet:

" • *I'm not ready*
- *I always make stupid mistakes*
- *I always run out of time*
- *I never do well on timed tests."*

This mental chatter was habitual with Roxanne ever since her early school days. Recognizing the "historical" nature of much of her self-talk encouraged her to consider how she might combat it.

Take time now to review your responses to Control Builders 3.1: What Did I Say? (p. 33) and 3.2: Ammunition Against My

Inner Critic (p. 36), to see how negative and positive self-talk might figure in your Stress Control Plan.

Step 4: Cultivate Positive Self-Talk

The easiest way to eradicate negative appraisals or destructive self-talk is to formulate opposing, positive statements. Roxanne listed three that she could repeat to herself during a timed test:

"• *I'm OK*
• *I am calm*
• *I know the material I'm being tested on.*"

It's important that your positive statements really are positive. For example, instead of saying, "I'm not going to panic," it's better to say, "I am calm." Positive self-talk is only one of several possible stress control techniques.

Step 5: Select Your Strategies

A stress control strategy is any activity that you can use to keep your stress at a manageable level. It need not be exotic. A successful stress control strategy can be as mundane as eating a leisurely breakfast, mentally complimenting yourself on your performance, or taking a few deep breaths before you make a phone call.

The Andrade Method uses seven possible stress control strategies:

- **Mental.** Because these are activities you do in your mind, they have the advantage of being portable and private.
- **Physical.** Activities that enhance your physical well-being will give you more stamina, make you more resilient, and lift your spirits.
- **Personal support.** Contact with living things—people, pets, even plants—enhances your self-esteem and helps you project a positive image when job hunting.
- **Emotional.** Acknowledging and expressing your emotions are essential to maintaining your mental and physical well-being.
- **Organizational.** These are activities that build structure into your personal life and job search.
- **Diversionary.** Taking a break from job hunting can restore your energy and help you to see your problems from a fresh perspective.
- **Spiritual.** Tending your inner life can help you maintain a sense of direction.

Figure 6.2 (pp. 73–74) lists examples of each of these strategies. Use it as inspiration to complete Control Builder 6.1: Stress Control Strategies I Can Use (p. 75). When brainstorming strategies, let your imagination run free: consider any and all resources that you have at your disposal. You will sift through them later to evaluate their appropriateness and the likelihood of their success.

Your first Stress Control Plans will be most effective if you rely on strategies that are already familiar to you and that you have used successfully in the past. Once your stress levels (and your job search) are under control, you can try adding new techniques to your repertoire.

For Step 5 of her Stress Control Plan Worksheet, Roxanne brainstormed the following strategies to try before, during, and after stressful interviews:

"Before:
- *Ask beforehand whether an interview involves a timed test; cancel interviews that do*
- *Practice taking tests with a timer*
- *Take a tranquilizer*
- *Be well rested before the interview.*

During:
- *Focus on positive thoughts before a test*
- *Use pleasant imagery to distract me from feeling anxious*
- *Set an alarm for halfway through the test*
- *Chant*
- *Breathe deeply while reading test*
- *Read the test through once before writing any answers.*

After:
- *Go for a walk*
- *Congratulate myself for having made it through the test*
- *Have a glass of wine*
- *Have a nap."*

Step 6: Evaluate Your Strategies

Once you have come up with your list of possible strategies, evaluate each for its appropriateness and probable effectiveness. Three questions will assist you in rating the usefulness of your strategies.

- Is this strategy a positive one, or will it cause further problems ?
- Is this strategy appropriate for me, the time, and the place?
- Am I using a short-term strategy when I really need one that is long-term?

FIGURE 6.2 The Seven Stress Control Strategies

TYPE OF STRATEGY	EXAMPLES
Mental	• Problem solve: take the situation apart, examine your options, develop a plan • Rehearse mentally: imagine yourself responding successfully • Look for a silver lining: find something positive in the situation • Psych yourself up: remind yourself of your strengths • Compliment yourself • Switch your self-talk from negative to positive • Recall a pleasant experience • Have a mental conversation with a supportive friend • Collect information that will help you solve a problem
Physical	• Do a relaxation exercise • Eat a low-fat, high-carbohydrate meal with lots of fresh vegetables • Have a nap • Dance • Get a massage • Exercise: walk, jog, cycle, skate, do aerobics, join an aqua-fit class, stretch, play a raquet sport, etc. • Have a glass of warm milk and some crackers • Soak in a warm bath • Play a team sport for enjoyment, not necessarily to win • Improve your grooming • Enjoy sex • Take a deep breath
Personal Support	• Go out with a friend • Talk to your partner • Play with children • Do volunteer work • Make a gift for a friend • Share a sport or a meal with someone • Nurture a plant • Rough-house with a pet • Join a club or special interest group • Write a letter to someone you care about • Spend leisure time with a friend
Emotional	• Hold your tongue if you think you are about to say something you'll regret • Pound a pillow • Feel your emotions, don't suppress them • Work off strong feelings with vigorous physical activity • Cry in the shower • Write a letter expressing your feelings to someone who has upset you, but don't mail it • Apologize for something you've done • Talk to a friend or counselor about your problems ☞

TYPE OF STRATEGY	EXAMPLES
Organizational	• Clean your work area • Make a "Things To Do" list before going to bed • Identify your priorities • Set yourself a time table • Break big tasks into smaller ones and start working on one small task • Balance your checkbook • Choose one important goal for the next six months • Sort your correspondence
Diversionary	• Watch something: a movie or play, sunset, birds • Collect something: stamps, leaves, books • Raise something: plants, pets • Build something: furniture, dolls, crafts, jigsaws • Listen to something: music, radio plays, books on cassette, birdsong • Pamper yourself: haircut, warm bath, good food • Walk in the rain • Go somewhere new (even in your own neighborhood) • Daydream • Read a book • Clean the house • Work on the car • Try something new
Spiritual	• Keep a journal of your thoughts • Watch the sun rise or set • Visit a park, conservation area, or garden • Read an inspirational poem or book • Meditate or say a prayer • Consider your special gifts and how you might use these to improve society • Spend a few moments at the end of the day giving thanks for the good things in your life • If you are religious, attend a place a worship, or talk to your spiritual guide • Remind yourself that this crisis is not the end of the world and that, regardless, the sun will rise tomorrow

Choose Positive Strategies

Some stress control strategies offer short-term relief and long-term problems. Relying on drugs or alcohol are two obvious examples. Yet even seemingly innocuous activities—such as exercise or fantasizing—can have negative effects on your personal life and job search if you use them to excess.

Questions to help you separate good from not-so-good stress control strategies might include

CONTROL 6.1 BUILDER

Stress Control Strategies I Can Use

(Use further sheets of paper as necessary.)

Type of Strategy	Strategies Available to Me
Mental	
Physical	
Personal Support	
Emotional	
Organizational	
Diversionary	
Spiritual	

- How often do I use this strategy—is it my main means of coping with stress?
- Might this strategy have negative consequences if I use it too frequently?
- Could I choose not to use it?

In Roxanne's case, two of her strategies were poor choices: tranquilizers and alcohol (individually would be bad enough, but together these can be lethal).

Use Strategies Appropriately

A good stress control strategy must be appropriate for the time and place you need to use it. While Roxanne found chanting aloud to be relaxing at home, she knew this would not be appropriate in public. She substituted an alternative: to repeat positive self-talk statements silently to herself.

Short-Term Versus Long-Term?

There is nothing intrinsically wrong with short-term stress control strategies. However, if you find yourself facing the same problem repeatedly, a longer-term solution—one that seeks and addresses the source of the problem—will be more beneficial.

In Roxanne's case, doing breathing exercises in the waiting room prior to the test was a useful short-term strategy. But this did not address her long-standing anxiety about test situations.

A longer-term strategy might include a few sessions with a counselor so that Roxanne could gain some insight into her low self-confidence and past negative experiences. A counselor could also coach her in further stress control techniques (such as helping her practice taking timed tests).

After evaluating her first list of stress control strategies, Roxanne decided to keep the following, which she listed in Step 6:

"Before:
- *Practice taking tests with a timer*
- *Be as well rested as possible before the test.*

During:
- *Repeat positive self-talk*
- *Use pleasant imagery to distract me from feeling anxious*
- *Breathe deeply while reading the test*
- *Set an alarm for halfway through the test*
- *Read the test through once without answering any questions, until I am calm enough to think clearly.*

After:
- *Go for a walk*
- *Congratulate myself for having made it through the test*
- *Have a nap."*

Step 7: Find Support for Your Plan

Don't deal with the stress of job hunting alone. Think about the kind of support (either material or moral) that might help you maintain your stress control strategies. Identify people whom you think could offer you this support.

Roxanne contacted her local Job Club to find out what help she might obtain there. Then, after discussing the alternatives with her best friend Jean, she filled in Step 7 of her Stress Control Plan Worksheet as follows:

"• *Go for practice timed tests at the Job Club*
• *Call Jean for a pep talk before and after an interview."*

Step 8: Test Your Plan

Give your plan a trial run to see how well it works. Ask yourself

- Did I get the result I wanted? Did this strategy help manage my stress?

If the answer is yes, then keep this part of your Stress Control Plan. If the answer is no, you will need to explore the reasons for the failure with the next two questions.

- Did my strategy fail because of the way I performed it (for example, breathing exercises)?
  If this was the case, you may need to practice the strategy before you attempt to use it again.
- Do I need to choose another strategy?

If your performance of the strategy was adequate, the problem may lie with the strategy itself. Not all strategies that appear to be useful may actually be effective in the crunch.

Don't be discouraged: the purpose of testing your Stress Control Plan is to weed out ineffective strategies. If you have any doubts about your choice of strategy, simply select another from your list.

Here is what Roxanne wrote for Step 8 of her Stress Control Plan Worksheet:

> "• *Setting an alarm, positive self-talk, reading the test through once: all helped; keep these.*
> • *Pleasant imagery was calming, but it took time and was distracting. Not a good choice for test situations.*
> • *Deep breathing helped, but I still find it difficult. Will practice and continue to use for awhile.*"

Step 9: Improve Your Plan

Knowing how your Stress Control Plan worked should help you to refine it. Don't hesitate to rethink your strategies. Your goal is to do better next time.

These were Roxanne's modifications for Step 9 of her Stress Control Plan Worksheet:

> "*Before:* • *Practice positive self-talk, deep breathing, taking tests with a timer*
> • *Be well rested.*
>
> *During:* • *Set alarm, read exam through once, continue deep breathing.*
>
> *After:* • *Go for a walk, congratulate myself, phone Jean.*"

Step 10: Write Yourself a Reminder

Keep your commitment—and your enthusiasm—strong by writing yourself an occasional reminder of what you are gaining through your Stress Control Plan. Here are two of Roxanne's entries from Step 10 of her Stress Control Plan Worksheet:

"April 1. Went to the Job Club today for practice tests. This is my first step in controlling my stress during interviews....

April 6. Took a real timed test today; found it easier to do breathing excercises. Am pleased that I can now recognize my signs and symptoms of stress and do something about them."

Now it's your turn. Work through the steps in Control Builder 6.2: My Stress Control Plan Worksheet (pp. 79-81) to create a plan of your own.

Congratulations—you have just created your first Stress Control Plan. As your job search progresses, return to Control Builder 6.2: My Stress Control Plan Worksheet as often as necessary to help you deal with stressors as they arise.

What's Next?

Move on to Chapter 7 to learn how relaxation techniques can complement your Stress Control Plan. Develop a personalized home relaxation program and conquer chronic job-search stress.

REMEMBER

- ✔ Learn to use stress control strategies before, during, and after a stress-provoking situation occurs.
- ✔ Effective stress control strategies are positive and appropriate to the situation in hand.
- ✔ Use the ten steps to stress control described in this chapter to structure your personalized Stress Control Plan. Be ready to reevaluate and improve your plan as your needs change.

CONTROL 6.2 BUILDER

My Stress Control Plan Worksheet

Follow these ten guidelines to complete your Stress Control Plan Worksheet.

1. Select one of your major stressors from Control Builder 5.1: My Worst Stressors (page 62). What is it about this situation that you find stressful? Place this stressor in the blank column opposite Step 1 ("The situation I find stressful...").
2. Review your personal signs and symptoms of stress as listed in Control Builder 5.2: My Stress Profile (page 63). Do any of these arise in the situation described in Step 1? List these (and any others) in the column opposite Step 2 ("My response/cues that I'm stressed...").
3. What is your negative self-talk in this situation? List this in the column opposite Step 3 ("My negative self-talk...").
4. For each negative statement, devise an opposing, positive statement and enter it in the column opposite Step 4 ("Positive statements I can use...").
5. Review the possible stress control resources you brainstormed in Control Builder 6.1 (page 75). Identify any that might address the stressor you listed in Step 1. Try to identify at least one intervention you might try before, during, and after the stressful event. List these opposite Step 5 ("Select my strategies...").
6. For each of the strategies you listed in Step 5, ask yourself: Is this a positive strategy? Is it appropriate for me in this place and at this time? Is it too short-term for the circumstances? Eliminate any negative or inappropriate strategies from your list and place the remaining ones opposite Step 6 ("Evaluate my strategies...").
7. In the column opposite Step 7 ("Find support for my plan..."), specify the kind of support you think you will need, and list the people or agencies that might provide it.
8. Seek an opportunity to test your Stress Control Plan. After your trial run, evaluate the success of your plan by asking yourself: Did this strategy help control my stress? If not, why not? Do I need a different strategy? Enter your assessment opposite Step 8 ("Test my plan").
9. Go back to the strategies you listed in Step 6. Can you improve or refine them? Feel free to discard or replace any that did not give the desired results. Place your revised strategies in the column opposite Step 9 ("My improved plan").
10. Review your Stress Control Plan Worksheet frequently. To reinforce your commitment, fill in occasional reminders in the column opposite Step 10. For example: What else have you learned about this stressor and your responses to it? Which strategies are most beneficial? Why?

☞

My Stress Control Plan Worksheet

Make as many photocopies of this blank worksheet as you think you'll need in order to create a plan that works for you. Use further sheets of paper as necessary.

Step 1: **Identify my stressor**	The situation I find stressful:	
Step 2: **Note my reaction**	My response/cues that I'm stressed:	
Step 3: **Spot negative self-talk**	My negative self-talk in this situation:	
Step 4: **Cultivate positive self-talk**	Positive statements I can use in this situation:	
Step 5: **Select my strategies**	Before: During: After:	

Step 6: **Evaluate my strategies**	Before: During: After:	
Step 7: **Find support for my plan**	Type of support I would like; people/agencies who can support me:	
Step 8: **Test my plan**	Before: During: After:	
Step 9: **My improved plan**	Before: During: After:	
Step 10: **My reminder to myself**	Date:	

Copyright © Carla-Krystin Andrade/Trifolium Books. Permission is granted to reproduce this worksheet for personal use only.

C H A P T E R

7

Learn to Relax

Many job hunters believe they cannot afford to take time to relax—and their job search suffers as a result.

Relaxation can become one of the secrets of your job-hunting success. This chapter tells you how. After looking at some common relaxation techniques, we'll discuss how you can set up your own home relaxation program.

What Is Relaxation?

What do *you* do when you want to relax—watch TV? Play squash? Have a nap? These activities may indeed be relaxing, but they are not relaxation in the strict sense of the word.

Relaxation is any technique that enables the body and brain to achieve a state of restfulness without entering a state of sleep. Such techniques produce physiological changes that are the opposite of those associated with the fight-or-flight response. These include

- Decreased heart rate
- Lower oxygen consumption
- Slower metabolic rate
- Decreased secretion of lactic acid into the blood (high blood lactate is associated with tension)
- Decreased tension in skeletal muscles
- Slower brain activity; increase in alpha brain waves
- Increased skin resistance to shock.

Relaxation Enhances Your Job Search

What effect does all this have on your job search? Plenty!

You already know that job hunting can be physically and mentally draining and extremely stressful. As we saw in Chapter 5, the symptoms of chronic stress undermine your ability to carry out your job-search tasks.

Research has shown that people who practice relaxation techniques on a regular basis experience

- Higher energy levels
- More productivity
- Better sleep
- Clearer thinking
- Better concentration and memory
- Greater emotional stability
- Less stress in demanding situations
- More calm and control
- Better all-around physical and mental health

than those who do not.

Relaxation is more than an escape from the stress in your life. Relaxation revitalizes you; it heals your mind and body. Given all the benefits, can any job hunter afford *not* to relax?

The "Competitive Edge"?

Some people believe that relaxation will hinder their job-search efforts. "I might lose my competitive edge," "I have to stay psyched up" are two arguments commonly given for avoiding relaxation. This perspective is misinformed.

The racing thoughts, muscular tension, and restlessness associated with job-search stress may initially make you feel primed and ready to spring from the starting block like a sprinter. But this revved-up "competitive edge" rapidly gives way to burnout, leaving you feeling lethargic and defeated—and unable to put your job-hunting skills to good use.

"Do I Need to Relax?"

Probably—if you've experienced two or more of the following signs in recent weeks:

- Needed more than one cup of coffee or tea to get you through the day
- Felt edgy and restless
- Had a panic attack—thoughts racing, heart pounding, palms sweating
- Lost your temper over something minor
- Burst into tears or felt very emotional for no clear reason
- Fell asleep while working
- Couldn't concentrate on your work
- Repeatedly lost or forgot things
- Lay awake at night watching the clock
- Took medication to sleep
- Couldn't unwind without an alcoholic drink
- Had a headache or stomachache

- Ran out of energy halfway through the day
- Felt frazzled and out of control
- Had an urge to scream, run away, or hide from your life.

You may have other signs unique to you that tell you when *you* need to relax. Even one sign is too many if you experience it frequently.

If you're not yet exhibiting any warning signs, now is the time to be proactive. Prevent developing them in the future by making time now for regular, structured relaxation. Your job search will benefit from it.

What's Out There?

This chapter describes a wide variety of relaxation methods. Some are mental techniques (autogenics, imagery, meditation), some involve physical control (biofeedback, breathing, progressive muscle relaxation), and some use movement (T'ai Chi Ch'uan and yoga). All produce the beneficial effects described above.

- **Autogenics**. The word means "self-generated," and was coined by J.H. Schultz, the psychiatrist who pioneered this form of deep relaxation in the 1920s. Autogenics uses mental imagery to counteract the major physical effects of stress. For example, you might learn to relax your stomach muscles by imagining that your solar plexus has become warm.
- **Biofeedback**. Short for "biological feedback," this technique uses electronic equipment to monitor stress-related physiological functions (e.g., heart rate; muscle action potentials). This feedback then enables you to control these functions at will—for example, slowing your heart rate and relaxing tense muscles.
- **Breathing exercises.** Deep, relaxed, diaphragmatic breathing is the basis of yoga and meditation. Breathing exercises increase the flow of oxygen to the blood and thereby help to eliminate toxins from the body. They also reverse the constrained breathing patterns caused by chronic stress.
- **Imagery and visualization.** *Not* mere daydreaming, these methods use specific images to achieve physical and mental relaxation. With guided imagery, you create pleasant mental scenes, such as a walk through a quiet forest. Visualization involves more abstract mental images, such as a soothing color.

- **Meditation.** Meditation involves focused contemplation upon a word or sound (such as a mantra), an image, or a thought. In the 1970s, Dr. Herbert Benson, a cardiologist, adapted meditation to create the Relaxation Response, in which mantras are replaced by short, commonly used English words, such as "one." The goal of meditation is to clear the mind of stress-provoking thoughts.
- **Progressive muscle relaxation.** Also known as Jacobson's technique (for Dr. Edmund Jacobson, the physiologist who developed it in the 1930s), this system involves alternately contracting and relaxing specific groups of muscles to produce overall relaxation. It also teaches you to distinguish between states of tension and relaxation—a distinction that you can lose when under chronic stress.
- **T'ai Chi Ch'uan.** Sometimes considered a "moving meditation," the various forms of T'ai Chi derive from ancient Chinese martial arts. T'ai Chi consists of a precise sequence of 108 slow, rhythmical movements. Graceful and flowing, this technique brings body and mind into harmony. It also makes the body stronger, more supple, and more relaxed.
- **Yoga.** The name derives from the Sanskrit word for "union." Hatha Yoga and Kundalini Yoga—the two forms best known in the West—use *asanas* (postures) and breathing exercises to achieve the goals of self-mastery and integration of body, mind, and spirit.

Which Technique Is Best?

Each of the above techniques has its advantages. No single method works equally well for everyone. Until you find a technique that suits you, you might wish to experiment with more than one.

The best relaxation technique is the one that gives you the results you want. It should suit *your* personality and interests, *your* learning style, and *your* resources.

Control Builder 7.1: Choose Your Relaxation Technique (pp. 86–87) lists some of the criteria you'll want to consider.

A Word About Aerobics

Strictly speaking, aerobic exercise (any activity that involves sustained, vigorous movement of the arms and legs and raises your heart rate) is not a relaxation technique. However, research does suggest that physical fitness training moderates the negative effects of stress and that physically fit people are less vulnerable to stress-related problems.

CONTROL 7.1 BUILDER

Choose Your Relaxation Technique

Part 1. As you read the questions below, circle any of the techniques in the "Yes" or "No" columns that seem appropriate to your situation.

Question	If Your Answer Is...	
	Yes	**No**
1. Do I need a technique I can do just about anywhere?	Autogenics Breathing Imagery Meditation Visualization • can be done almost anywhere	Biofeedback Progressive relaxation T'ai Chi Yoga • are less portable, require a specific place
2. Do I find it difficult to sit or lie still?	T'ai Chi Yoga • involve movement	Autogenics Biofeedback Breathing Imagery Meditation Progressive relaxation Visualization • are generally done sitting or lying still
3. Do I want to still racing thoughts?	Imagery Meditation Visualization • address this need most specifically	All techniques are ultimately beneficial in this respect.
4. Do I want to recognize when my muscles are tense?	Biofeedback Progressive relaxation Yoga • specifically teach awareness of tension/relaxation	Autogenics Breathing Imagery Meditation T'ai Chi Visualization • do not work directly with muscular tension
5. Do I form mental images easily?	Autogenics Imagery Meditation Visualization • maximize this ability	Biofeedback Breathing Progressive relaxation T'ai Chi Yoga • do not require visualization skills

☞

Question	If Your Answer Is...	
	Yes	**No**
6. Do I have the patience to learn a technique that involves many different steps?	Progressive relaxation T'ai Chi Yoga • involve a sequence of steps or movements	Autogenics Biofeedback Breathing Imagery Meditation Visualization • usually do not involve sequential steps
7. Do I have a practice space that is quiet?	Autogenics Biofeedback Imagery Meditation Visualization • are more enjoyable when practiced in a quiet place	Breathing Progressive relaxation T'ai Chi Yoga • do not require quiet
8. Do I have a practice space large enough to move around in?	T'ai Chi Yoga • require space to move	Other techniques are generally done sitting or lying.

Part 2. In your responses to Part 1, which technique(s) did you circle most often? Which technique looks as though it might best suit your needs? (If most of your responses fall in the "Yes" column, consider beginning with one or more of these techniques.)

____

____

____

____

____

____

____

Regular aerobic exercise is a healthy, stress-relieving practice. Yet, while long-distance running, swimming, or cycling may give you a peaceful feeling, a noisy aerobics class will not provide the inner calm and physical relaxation of the techniques described above.

What About My Stress Control Plan?

The Stress Control Plan that you developed in Control Builder 6.2 (pp. 79–81) helps you organize and evaluate the strategies you can use to prevent and overcome stress-provoking situations.

Relaxation techniques, on the other hand, are stress control strategies that directly alleviate the physiological and psychological signs of stress. Relaxation is actually the most important stress control strategy you can use.

Your Stress Control Plan is *not* interchangeable with the relaxation techniques described in this chapter. Rather, each complements the other. Making relaxation a part of your daily routine will make your Stress Control Plan more effective.

How Do I Find Out About Relaxation?

Here are answers to some common questions about relaxation.

Must I Learn from an Instructor?

No; you can teach yourself to relax. Your success will depend on the technique you choose, your comfort with teach-yourself methods, and your commitment to learning. If you're not sure what's best for you, consider at least starting out with an instructor.

Your local "Y" may offer courses in one or more relaxation techniques. You might also check the classified section of your local newspaper, or look under "Stress Management" in the Yellow Pages. Instructors in relaxation techniques neither receive nor offer standardized training programs. When checking out a particular school or clinic, always ask what training they require of their teaching staff. Find out whether the instructor will be using relaxation tapes—if so, you may do just as well on your own. And make sure you like the environment where you'll be learning to relax.

How May I Learn Relaxation on My Own?

Many relaxation techniques can be learned from books, video tapes, and audio cassettes. Biofeedback is a notable exception because it requires specialized equipment and supervised training.

In shopping for books or tapes, keep these pointers in mind:

- Does the book or tape give clear instructions?
- Do you find the voice on the tape soothing?
- Is the pacing of the tape too fast or too slow?

- How long is the tape (or the routine)? Will it fit into your schedule? Can you modify it?
- Does the tape have music that might be distracting or irritating?

Wherever possible, listen or watch before you buy.

Note: Subliminal tapes (those that you listen to while sleeping or doing some other activity) will *not* teach you how to do relaxation techniques.

What's My Learning Style?

If you feel self-conscious about relaxation, find a sympathetic instructor and a learning environment that offers some privacy. On the other hand, you may enjoy the social aspect of group instruction. Investigate your options, and choose the learning approach that is most familiar and comfortable to you.

How Much Does Relaxation Training Cost?

Popular techniques, such as yoga and T'ai Chi, are often available at low cost through community centers. One-on-one lessons cost more than group instruction.

You can learn to relax without spending another cent, by using the self-study techniques suggested later in this chapter. Or you can borrow audio or video tapes on relaxation at your local library. Paying more doesn't necessarily mean you will derive greater benefit. So shop around for instruction that is within your budget.

Where Can I Relax?

Contrary to popular belief, you need not practice relaxation in a silent, dark room. You want a convenient method that you can practice at home (and perhaps in other locations) as part of your daily routine.

Some methods can be done virtually anywhere. Others, like yoga and T'ai Chi, require space for movement, such as a park, gym, or your living room.

How Long Do I Relax?

Twenty minutes a day is a general rule of thumb, although the time required for specific techniques will vary.

Considering the benefits to be gained from relaxing, twenty minutes is not a big investment of time—only 1.4 percent of your day. That's probably less time than you spend brewing coffee.

Are Relaxation Techniques Safe?

Relaxation is safe for virtually everyone. Some techniques, such as guided imagery and progressive muscle relaxation, are routinely taught to people who are coping with chronic or life-threatening illness.

A word of caution, however: Each technique has its own physical and psychological requirements and effects. If you have special needs—any condition that affects your physical or psychological function—it is recommended that you begin relaxation training with a qualified instructor who is familiar with your condition.

If you have back pain, shortness of breath, arthritis, depression, or are pregnant, consult your health care practitioner before beginning your relaxation program.

Begin Your Home Relaxation Program

Your relaxation program will be most successful when it is a basic part of your daily routine. To make this happen, you need to consider

- Time
- Place
- Clothing
- Position
- Your attitude.

Time

There is no single ideal time to relax. Experiment until you find *your* best time. Here are a few guidelines:

- Do relaxation exercises at around the same time each day.
- Don't schedule relaxation right after meals. Relax either before meals, or one or two hours after to allow proper digestion.
- Avoid times when you are likely to fall asleep. Sleep is not the same as relaxation.
- Don't do relaxation exercises just prior to going to bed. Many people are energized by relaxation.

Consider relaxing at those times of the day when you feel most sluggish or stressed. This can give you the energy to get through a slump.

Place

Attempting to do T'ai Chi in a cramped, cluttered bedroom is frustrating. So is trying to do full-body progressive relaxation while standing on a crowded bus! Your relaxation space should be

- Large enough to sit, lie, or move in, as your technique demands
- Comfortably warm
- Reasonably well ventilated
- As quiet as your technique requires (quiet is less important as your skill at relaxation improves).

Clothing

Most relaxation techniques do not require special clothes. Your clothing should be comfortable: loose enough not to constrict your breathing or circulation, and heavy enough to keep you warm.

Because your body becomes cooler as it slows down during relaxation, you may wish to keep a light blanket handy.

Position

Relaxation may be practiced sitting or lying (see Figures 7.1 and 7.2). Lying supine (on the back) allows fuller, easier breathing. But if this position is uncomfortable for you, then try sitting.

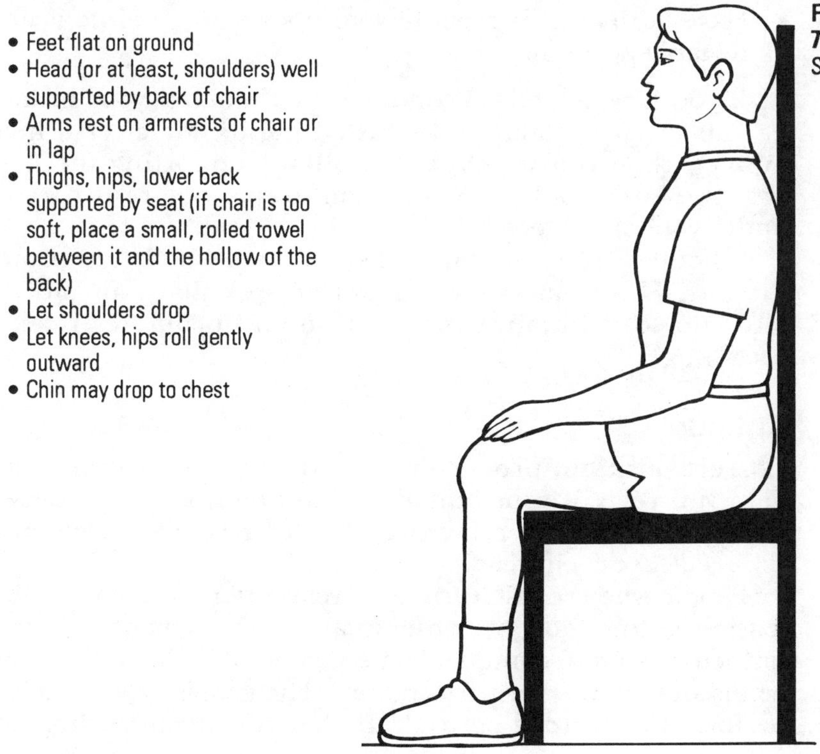

FIGURE 7.1 Sitting

FIGURE 7.2
Lying

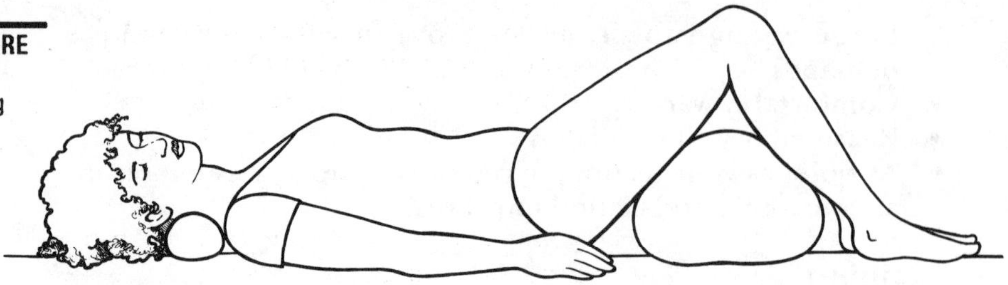

- Face towards ceiling
- Head supported with small pillow (to fit curve of the neck without causing it to bend)
- Larger pillow under bent knees (to relax lower back)
- Hands on pelvis or at sides
- Shoulders, heels on mat
- Knees, hips roll gently outward

If you are pregnant, you will be more comfortable lying on your side. In this case

- Bend both your knees and hips to 90 degrees
- Place a medium-sized pillow between your knees
- Support the curve of your neck with a small pillow
- Have both arms in front of your body and bent into a comfortable position.

If you have a medical condition that requires your head to be raised (for example, in gastric reflux, or after a head injury), then replace the small pillow supporting the neck with two larger pillows. Stack them so that one rests partially under your shoulders.

Whether sitting or lying, make sure your body has proper support. This reduces the amount of work that your muscles must do to maintain your position and promotes relaxed breathing.

Attitude

Correct position, proper dress, and suitable location won't help you relax if your attitude creates tension. Some people struggle so hard to relax that they experience Relaxation-Induced Anxiety instead.

People who are just learning to relax often find that physical tension, racing thoughts, or unusual sensations make it difficult to focus on the technique. Some people fall asleep. But don't be discouraged by early frustrations. The goal is to relax, not to perform the exercise perfectly. If after correct instruction and diligent practice a particular technique still does not work for you, then consider another, or a combination of techniques.

Above all, be patient with yourself.

Time to Relax!

Three simple techniques you can try on your own include breathing exercises, progressive muscle relaxation, and imagery. Before you begin, you need to understand the mechanics of breathing.

Diaphragmatic Breathing

Children naturally use diaphragmatic or "stomach" breathing. By adulthood, most people have acquired poor breathing habits, and their breathing becomes shallower as a result (this is encouraged by fashion trends that constrict the midsection).

Figure 7.3(a) shows the *diaphragm*, a dome-shaped muscle that spans the bottom of the ribcage, sealing the chest cavity. When your diaphragm expands fully, as in Figure 7.3(b), this increases the space available for your lungs to expand.

Not utilizing your diaphragm fully leads to tense, shallow breathing and limits the amount of oxygen you inhale. It is oxygen that removes wastes and toxins from your body, including those that build up as the result of chronic stress.

Although it's sometimes called "stomach" breathing, diaphragmatic breathing has nothing to do with your stomach. Simply pushing your stomach in and out will not activate your diaphragm. To learn diaphragmatic breathing, try the four steps that follow on page 94.

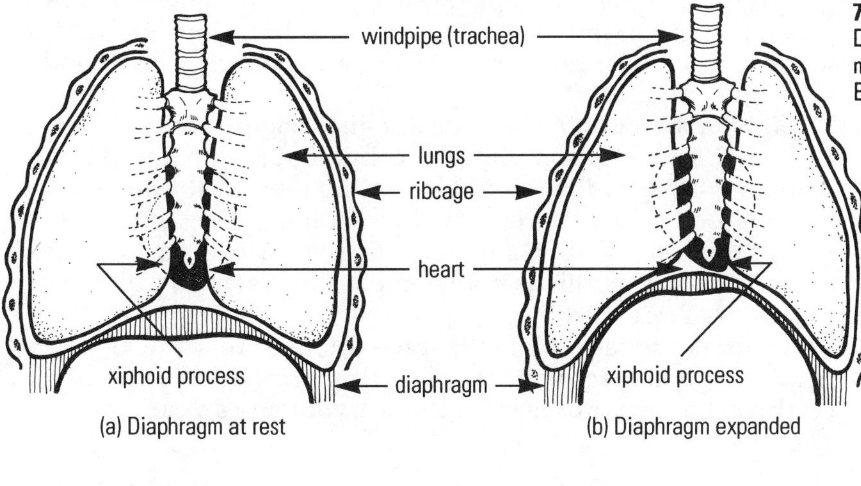

FIGURE 7.3 Diaphragmatic Breathing

- Sit or lie comfortably.
- Run the fingers of each of your hands up along the lower border of your ribcage until they meet in the notch at the center, over your stomach. This is your *xiphoid process.* Place the thumb of one hand in this notch and let the rest of your hand sit gently on your abdomen. (Don't let your hand slip down.)
- Close your eyes, take a slow breath in through your nose, imagine the air flowing into your lungs, and feel the hand resting over your xiphoid process rise as your chest expands.
- Sigh the air out through your mouth.

If you can't feel your hand rising, don't attempt to take bigger breaths. This will only encourage you to tense and raise your shoulders, and defeats the purpose of the exercise. Instead, take longer, slower breaths to give your lungs time to fill with air.

Diaphragmatic breathing takes practice. Be patient with yourself as you apply it in the breathing exercises that follow. As your ability to relax improves, it will feel more natural.

Breathing Exercises

Time: 5-10 minutes
Position: Lying or sitting
Equipment: None

Home Instructions:
Try one or more of the following exercises, using the technique for diaphragmatic breathing described above.

- **Just breathe**. The simplest of all, you can do this one anywhere—which makes it perfect for interviews, long line-ups, and other stress-provoking moments. There are two steps: (1) Choose a comfortable position, then (2) take a deep breath in and sigh the air out through your mouth. Repeat as needed.
- **Sigh tension out.** As you breathe in, imagine yourself filling your body with a feeling of calm. Then sigh the air out through your mouth and picture the tension flowing out of your body with the expelled air. Allow your body to sink further into your chair, mat, or bed at the end of each breath. Repeat this as many times as necessary up to a maximum of ten minutes.
- **Trace the breath.** Mentally trace the path that the air takes as you breathe. Inhale, picturing the air as it flows in through your nose, moves down your windpipe, and fills

your lungs. Then retrace its flow until you sigh it out through your mouth.

From there, you can imagine the air "entering" different parts of your body: flowing down to your stomach, your pelvis, your legs, your toes.

- **Count breaths.** This exercise involves counting mentally from 1 to 10 as you breathe. For the first cycle, as you inhale, think "1"; sigh the air out and and mentally repeat "1." Then inhale, thinking "2"; sigh the air out and think "2." Repeat until you reach 10. Then count backwards in the same fashion until you return to 1.

  For the second cycle, count only as you exhale: breathe in, then sigh the air out and think "1"; breathe in, then sigh the air out and think "2." Continue until you have counted to 10, and then count backwards to 1.

  Repeat these two cycles as many times as necessary up to a maximum of ten minutes.

Common Pitfall:
Anxiety, or a feeling that the breathing is getting out of control.

We're not accustomed to thinking about breathing—so breathing exercises are by definition a little unnatural. With practice, you'll become more comfortable focusing on the breath. If you find yourself growing anxious, stop the exercise. Take the mind off the breathing for a moment, and resume when you feel able.

Progressive Muscle Relaxation

Time: Short form, 5-10 minutes; full-body, 20 minutes
Position: Lying or sitting
Equipment: None

Home Instructions:
Progressive muscle relaxation (also called Jacobson's technique) can be done in two ways: the full-body form or the short form. Emphasize whichever muscle groups you wish. Sample sequences:

- Full-body form: Relax hands - shoulders - neck - face - chest - buttocks - thighs - calves - feet.
- Short form: Relax hands - shoulders - neck - face (only).

For each group of muscles, follow this general sequence:
1. Tighten the muscle(s).
2 Focus on how uncomfortable the tension there is.
3. Hold the tension (but not so much that it hurts).
4. Slowly release the tension.

5. Focus on the muscles as they become looser and more relaxed.
6. Notice the difference between this feeling of relaxation and the tension that was in the muscle(s) before.
7. Allow the newly relaxed muscle(s) to sink into the mat or chair.

Here are some physical cues to help you focus on each muscle group.

- **Hands and forearms.** Clench your fists and squeeze them tight; hold and release.
- **Shoulders.** Lift your shoulders up to your ears; hold and release.
- **Neck.** Push your head back into the pillow or chair, or squeeze your chin against your chest; hold and release.
- **Face.** Scrunch your face up: wrinkle your forehead, squeeze your eyes shut, clench your teeth, push your tongue up against the roof of your mouth. Hold and release.
- **Chest.** Take a deep breath in and hold. You'll feel tension building in your chest. Hold the tension briefly. Then sigh the air out through your mouth to release the tension.
- **Buttocks.** Tighten the muscles of your bottom and hold; release.
- **Thighs.** Pull your toes up towards your nose; straighten your knees and lift your feet off the bed or floor. Hold legs straight, then release.
- **Calves.** Point your toes and feet like a ballet dancer; hold and release.
- **Feet.** Curl your toes as tight as you can; hold and release.

Common Pitfall:
Difficulty letting tension in muscles go; forgetting instructions.

Be sure to release muscles after each contraction, and to pause so that you can feel the relaxation in that group of muscles before proceeding to the next group. If having trouble remembering instructions, ask a friend to read the sequence aloud to you.

Imagery

Time: 10-20 minutes
Position: Lying or sitting
Equipment: None

Home Instructions:
Imagery exercises are like creating movies in your mind. Rather than static pictures, you want images that are fluid, rich, and real. Here is a suggested sequence:

1. Sit or lie comfortably and take a few deep breaths before you begin.

2. Visualize your movie's "opening shot." Pick a pleasant and calming place, and mentally take yourself there.
3. Use all five senses in creating your scene. What can you hear, see, smell, feel, and taste? Involving your senses may trigger memory; for example, imagining the smell of pine trees may remind you of an actual hiking trip.
4. Let your scene unfold. What happens next? Where do you go? What do you do? Take time to enjoy the calming scene you have created.
5. Bring yourself back—but not too quickly. Picture yourself slowly leaving your scene. Then focus on your relaxed body. Finally, take a deep breath and give yourself a few moments to gather your thoughts.

For starters, try some of these images:

- **Beach scene.** You are lying on a silvery beach. The sky above is clear and blue. The sun warms your body, and the sand beneath you is soft and warm against your skin. You can taste the salt in the air; you can smell the ocean. You hear the splash of waves rolling onto the shore. Your tension flows out to sea with the waves.
- **Forest walk.** You are walking in a peaceful forest. The sun shines on your face through a tangle of leaves. You hear the birds twittering and the wind sighing through the trees. The moss on the ground is soft and damp under your feet. You sit in a small clearing fragrant with pine and juniper, and feel at peace.
- **Bubbling brook.** You stroll beside a crystal-clear brook as it bubbles over the stones. The gentle gurgling of the water is soothing. You sit cooling your feet in the brook, and the water washes your tension away.
- **Field of flowers.** You sit in the midst of a field of flowers. All around you are blossoms of every possible color and shape. You hear the flowers rustling in the breeze. Their soft petals brush against your skin, and the air is filled with their exotic perfume. As you breathe in the scent of the flowers, you sigh all the tension out of your body.

Common Pitfall:
Unwanted thoughts; difficulty maintaining images.

As you relax, your conscious mental barriers are lowered and your thoughts tend to wander. If you don't fight these thoughts, they will likely pass as readily as they came. Simply recreate your image, and pick up the "story" where you left off.

You Can't Afford Not to Relax

Breathing exercises, progressive muscle relaxation, and imagery are just three of the relaxation techniques you can teach yourself at home. Or consider taking a course in any of the other methods discussed in this chapter. Control Builder 7.2 will help you formulate your relaxation plan.

Relaxation can improve your energy levels, sharpen your concentration, and enhance your physical and mental health. With relaxation as a regular part of your job-hunting routine, you'll be able to work longer and more effectively. Most important of all, you'll feel calmer and more in control of your life and your job search. And all this in as little as twenty minutes a day!

What's Next?

By now, you have tried at least one relaxation technique to get your stress levels under control. Move on to Stage 3 to learn how to get the most out of each day of your job search.

REMEMBER

- ✔ Relaxation produces physiological changes that are opposite to those of the fight-or-flight response.
- ✔ There is no single best relaxation technique. The best method is one that suits your personality and resources.
- ✔ The goal of relaxation is to feel calmer, not to perform the technique perfectly. Don't work too hard at relaxing—that defeats the purpose.
- ✔ Relaxation is safe for virtually everyone. However, people with special physical and psychological needs should consult their health care practitioner before beginning a relaxation program.

CONTROL 7.2 BUILDER

My Relaxation Plan

Once you are ready to begin your relaxation program, use this log to track your progress. Make a separate log for each relaxation technique that you try.

Technique I've chosen	
Time of day I'll relax	
Equipment I'll need	
If taking a course, where and when will it meet?	
Do I still like this technique after one week?	
Am I having problems with this technique? If so, what are they?	
How might I address these problems?	
Other notes	

Copyright © Carla-Krystin Andrade/Trifolium Books. Permission is granted to reproduce this page for personal use only.

Stage 3

Make Each Day Count

The chapters you have worked through so far have given many practical hints and exercises to help you

- Take stock of your current situation
- Set and prioritize your goals
- Rebuild your self-image and self-confidence
- Fight criticism
- Build a Stress Control Plan
- Begin a home relaxation program.

How can you organize all these hints and plans into your day?

The chapters in Stage 3 will show you how to get the most out of each day of your job search. They focus on some of the obstacles faced daily by job hunters. You'll learn how to

- Change your current bedtime and morning routines to improve your mornings
- Use your Stress Control Plan to respond more calmly and effectively to daily problems
- Use rewards and relaxation to make your evenings more enjoyable
- Design a better daily routine following the Daily Control Plan, and put it into action.

CHAPTER 8

The Daily Control Plan

How would you describe your job-hunting days? Are they productive, rewarding, invigorating?

If you are like most job hunters, too many of your days may seem plagued by a never-ending series of obstacles—like those experienced by Frank and Marquita.

The days drag by for Frank, a commodities trader who suddenly found himself out of work when his company downsized six months ago. Now he finds it difficult to get motivated to do the basics—meals, household chores, getting out of the house. Awake until 4 a.m. and asleep until late in the afternoon, Frank has become a reclusive night owl: even being with friends takes too much energy. He knows he's in a slump, but doesn't know how to get out of it.

Life has become a roller coaster ride for Marquita since she immigrated in search of better opportunities as a software developer. Now, she runs around all day, feeling scrambled and out of control. Short-tempered, irritable, and defensive, Marquita has become more impatient and critical. She tries to stay organized, but is easily thrown off balance by little things. Night after night, Marquita lies awake, trying to stop her racing thoughts and wishing that life would slow down.

Figure 8.1 compares Frank's day with Marquita's. Are there any similarities between their days and yours?

A Day in the Life of a Job Hunter

On the surface, Frank and Marquita seem very different. However, they share something in common: both suffer from too much stress and too little structure, the two most common pitfalls facing job hunters.

Fortunately, Frank and Marquita are not necessarily doomed to have stressful, unstructured days forever. None of their problems are insurmountable. And neither are yours.

LIKE FRANK?	LIKE MARQUITA?
• Lethargic • Unmotivated • Isolated • Unproductive • Depressed • Directionless	• Disorganized • Frantic • Easily flustered • Irritable • Out of control • Pressured

FIGURE 8.1 How Do You Spend Your Day?

Too Much Stress

Both Frank and Marquita are showing signs of chronic stress. Marquita's is the experience most often associated with stress—irritability, disorganization, excessive activity, racing thoughts, and a feeling of being out of control. Frank, however, is no less stressed than Marquita. Depression, lethargy, and social withdrawal are common in people who are under chronic stress.

Neither Frank nor Marquita has incorporated principles of stress control into his or her day. As a result, they have moved well beyond the "good" stress zone discussed in Chapter 5 and into the realm of chronic stress.

Too Little Structure

Job hunters must run a daily gauntlet of new tasks and experiences. Many have recently undergone the loss of a job or some other drastic change of routine, such as graduating from school.

Regardless of the reasons for their job search, most job hunters tend to make one of two errors in responding to change:

- They don't adjust their old routine to include time for new job-hunting tasks
- They don't replace a lost routine.

Adjust Your Old Routine

Some job hunters do not anticipate just how complex and time-consuming a job search will be. As a result, they struggle to keep up their usual routine while performing a new roster of job-search tasks. These people end up feeling stressed and overextended, because there never seem to be enough hours in the day to accomplish all that they must do.

Planning a successful job search means rethinking your daily routine. Ensuring that your routine is realistic—that the activities you have planned are actually achievable in a twenty-four-hour period—may also mean discarding some activities that are less important.

If your old routine no longer suits your current circumstances, there is little point in hanging on to it.

Replace Your Lost Routine

Losing your job or graduating from school can spell a sudden and radical change—or loss—of routine. Most people don't adhere to a strict timetable of daily activities. But we all need some degree of routine to give our life structure.

If you aren't used to scheduling your time, you may not even realize that you have lost a routine. Failure to replace a lost routine can leave you wandering aimlessly through each day of your job search.

If you are currently unemployed, you may find that the people in your life don't value your time because they think you have more free time than they have. As a result, they may make greater demands on you for errands and household chores. While these activities offer a kind of routine, they will leave you less time to work on your job search.

Routine Adds Structure and Meaning

A lack of structure—no routine or an unrealistic routine—leaves you without a foundation upon which to build your job search. Your days become a blur—weekdays, weekends, holidays all seem the same. This can lead to

- Feelings of confusion and loss of purpose
- A sense of having time on your hands
- Loss of control of your time
- Increased vulnerability to stress.

It's impossible to maintain a well-organized and efficient job search when you're experiencing these problems. On the other hand, a realistic, thoughtful routine

- Adds structure to your life
- Encourages you and others to value your time
- Allows you to balance work and leisure
- Helps you work more efficiently and achieve your goals
- Decreases your stress.

Evaluating your old routine and building a new one is not a complicated process. But it does take time and motivation.

The Daily Control Plan

The Andrade Method uses a three-stage Daily Control Plan (Figure 8.2) to organize all the activities that make up your day. It groups your activities according to the time of the day in which you usually do them. The three stages—Get Off to a Good Start (night before and morning), Hang In There (daytime), and Go for a Strong Finish (evening)—act as signposts. They remind you when it's time to close one stage of your day and move on to the next.

This chapter outlines the Daily Control Plan. Then, each of the next three chapters explores one stage of the Plan and suggests activities to include in each.

Don't try to make immediate, major changes in your existing routine. Instead, read through the next three chapters and complete the Control Builders, gradually laying the foundation for a successful daily routine.

Get Off to a Good Start

This is the beginning of your day of job hunting. Every day of your job search allows you to begin afresh. You put the previous day's successes and disappointments behind you and focus on what's ahead.

It's important to begin each day as you hope to finish. Get organized, set your goals, and begin every day with purpose and enthusiasm. When you do these things, you remind yourself that you are capable of tackling the day ahead.

FIGURE 8.2 The Daily Control Plan

Hang In There

Once you're headed in the right direction, your task is to get through your day with the help of the techniques and resources that you now have, such as your Stress Control Plan from Chapter 6.

Because the Daily Control Plan focuses on only one day at a time, you never feel you have to achieve *all* your goals, eliminate *all* your stress, or make sudden, drastic changes in your life.

Hang In There focuses on specific, manageable activities that free you from unrealistic expectations of perfection and the accompanying unnecessary pressure.

Go for a Strong Finish

Don't end your day feeling exhausted and defeated. The final stage of the Daily Control Plan shows you how to catch your second wind and pull yourself together at the end of your job-hunting day. Remind yourself of your successes. Finish each day with the enthusiasm and determination with which you began.

Build a New Routine

Log Your Days

To improve your days, you need to know exactly how you spend them. As well as the problem spots, you want to identify those parts of your day that work well. Then, you can concentrate on changing only the things that really need to be changed.

A daily log is a simple way to track where your time goes. Figure 8.3 shows a sample. Record how you use *your* time in Control Builder 8.1: My Daily Log (p. 108).

Recording your activities may seem like a lot of work, but it is a worthwhile exercise. You cannot make your days more effective until you spot your weak points. A few hints for making this exercise easier:

- Don't write down every single thing you do during the day—concentrate on the main activities.
- If you find it difficult to remember what you've done, photocopy your Daily Log and carry it around with you. Take a short break every few hours and fill it in.
- An alternative to a written log might be an audio cassette recording. Then you can either work from the tape, or copy what you recorded onto the Daily Log.

FIGURE 8.3 Sample Daily Log

TIME	ACTIVITY
6:00-7:00 a.m.	*n/a*
7:00-8:00	*7:15 Wake up; get out of bed; shower; dress*
8:00-9:00	*Cook breakfast; make lunch for kids; get organized for errands*
9:00-10:00	*Take kids to school; buy newspaper*
10:00-11:00	*Travel to Job Club*
11:00-12:00	*At Job Club*
12:00-1:00 p.m.	*Lunch*
1:00-2:00	*Errands*
2:00-3:00	*Home; nap*
3:00-4:00	*Kids home*
4:00-5:00	*Supervise homework*
5:00-6:00	*Make dinner*
6:00-7:00	*Eat dinner; clean up*
7:00-8:00	*TV; return phone calls*
8:00-9:00	*Kids to bed*
9:00-10:00	*Write cover letters for résumés*
10:00-11:00	*Snack; read*
11:00-12:00	*11:30 Bed*

Draft Your Plan

Once you've logged your activities for a couple of days, you're ready to outline your Daily Control Plan—the bare bones of your new routine. You will make the strong points of your current schedule the foundation for each Daily Control Plan you draw up in the future. (You won't have to repeat the Daily Log or the reorganization steps.)

CONTROL 8.1 BUILDER

My Daily Log

Keep track of your activities for one or two days. Describe them in as much detail as you wish.

Time	Activity
6:00-7:00 a.m.	
7:00-8:00	
8:00-9:00	
9:00-10:00	
10:00-11:00	
11:00-12:00	
12:00-1:00 p.m.	
1:00-2:00	
2:00-3:00	
3:00-4:00	
4:00-5:00	
5:00-6:00	
6:00-7:00	
7:00-8:00	
8:00-9:00	
9:00-10:00	
10:00-11:00	
11:00-12:00	

Copyright © Carla-Krystin Andrade/Trifolium Books. Permission is granted to reproduce this page for personal use only.

Take Your Day Apart

Go through the time slots of your completed Daily Log with a colored pen or pencil.

- Circle the points of your day that run smoothly. These are the time slots that won't need many changes.
- Put an asterisk beside the activities that you think are important to your routine. They may not be in the correct time slot at the moment, but they are the activities that you want to make a part of every day: meals, domestic chores, job-search tasks, leisure time.
- Put a large X through any blocks of time that are free to use for other activities.

Build on Your Strengths

Next, complete Control Builder 8.2 (p. 110), which looks like the Daily Log, to create the outline for your Daily Control Plan. First, photocopy the blank Plan. Then work in pencil and keep an eraser handy; you'll be moving things around in later steps.

How to Fill in the Plan

- Start with the time slots on your Daily Log that already run smoothly. Copy the activities in these time slots onto your Daily Control Plan.
- Look at those blocks of time on your Daily Log that you marked with a large X. Put a small x in the corner of these time slots on your Daily Control Plan, to show that these are free.
- Go through the activities on your Daily Log that you marked with an asterisk because they are important. Decide approximately how long each takes, and when you might best get it done. Did you write any of these activities into your Daily Control Plan in step 1? If not, slot them in now, in those free slots marked with a small x.

What you have now is a rough outline for your day. This Daily Control Plan is one you can use tomorrow. After that, each day will require changes to accommodate your commitments of that day.

The next three chapters explore the steps of the Daily Control Plan to keep you in control of your day. The first time through, these steps may seem painstaking. But after you've gone through the process once or twice, you'll move more quickly through each step.

CONTROL 8.2 BUILDER

My Daily Control Plan

Time	Activity
6:00-7:00 a.m.	
7:00-8:00	
8:00-9:00	
9:00-10:00	
10:00-11:00	
11:00-12:00	
12:00-1:00 p.m.	
1:00-2:00	
2:00-3:00	
3:00-4:00	
4:00-5:00	
5:00-6:00	
6:00-7:00	
7:00-8:00	
8:00-9:00	
9:00-10:00	
10:00-11:00	
11:00-12:00	

Today's Stressors

Action Plan

Copyright © Carla-Krystin Andrade/Trifolium Books. Permission is granted to reproduce this page for personal use only.

Keep It Simple

When building your Daily Control Plan, begin by thinking in terms of a general structure that will suit most days. A sound routine is

- Uncomplicated
- Easy to remember
- Simple to put into action.

This doesn't mean that every day of your week is going to be the same. What you're laying down is just the framework for your days. Once your general routine is in place, you can tailor each day to fit the activities on hand.

Include Stress Control Strategies

As we have seen in previous chapters, stress control is too important to be left to chance. Keep yourself squarely in the "good" stress zone. Anticipate the stressors you may encounter over the coming day, and record at least one strategy for dealing with each in your Daily Control Plan (see your responses to Control Builder 6.2: My Stress Control Plan Worksheet, pp. 80–81).

Keep Picking Yourself Up

If you find yourself becoming overwhelmed or getting off track at any point during the day, don't panic. All is not lost.

Stop. Remember the Daily Control Plan, and remind yourself which part of the day you have reached. Get on with *one specific activity* that belongs in this particular time of day. You'll get through the cycle as long as you keep picking yourself up when you stumble.

Make your Daily Control Plan the foundation of your job-hunting day. It's a simple cycle for an organized, productive, and enjoyable day of job hunting.

What's Next?

To refine your Daily Control Plan, move on to Chapter 9, which investigates how to Get Off to a Good Start and begin each day in a positive, organized manner.

REMEMBER

- ✔ The two most common pitfalls of job hunting are too much stress and too little structure.
- ✔ Having a daily routine gives your days structure and meaning and allows you to organize a more effective job search.
- ✔ Two common job-search errors include not adjusting an old routine to suit current circumstances and not replacing a lost routine.
- ✔ A written plan is essential to making good use of your time, in your personal life as well as your job search.
- ✔ The ideal job-hunting routine is one that plans one day at a time, is simple to use, and includes stress control strategies.

CHAPTER

9

Get Off to a Good Start

Are you a "morning person"? Do you bounce out of bed and greet the new day with a smile? Or do you drag yourself from bed, bleary-eyed, cursing those people who can't hide their morning cheer?

Even if you're not at your best before noon, you can learn to Get Off to a Good Start—the first stage of the Daily Control Plan—and thereby get more out of your mornings.

FIGURE 9.1 The Daily Control Plan

Mornings Can Be a Disaster

Many things can get your job-hunting day off to a bad start. Witness the morning routine of Marquita, our friend from Chapter 8.

> *Marquita wakes with a start as the alarm goes off. She has spent another restless night, lying awake for hours before falling into a fitful sleep troubled by nightmares. Now there's just enough time to get dressed and catch the 8:30 bus. As Marquita stumbles into the shower, the phone rings. It's about today's interview, which she forgot to confirm. She dresses while talking on the phone and skips breakfast. Briefcase in hand, Marquita runs for the bus, feeling as though she has left something behind. Later, she remembers that the notes for this morning's interview are still sitting on the dining room table. "It's going to be one of those days," she groans.*

Mornings would be less stressful for Marquita if she were to get organized the night before.

The Night Before

Many people think that a low-stress day begins in the morning. But there are three steps you can take the night before to help lower your morning stress levels and increase your sense of control during the day:

- Step 1: Plan Your Next Day
- Step 2: Prepare for Hassles
- Step 3: Don't Take Your Stress to Bed.

Step 1: Plan Your Next Day

How often do you end your day without having accomplished the one thing you absolutely had to do? To avoid this, plan your day the night before. Decide what you wish to achieve the next day, then evaluate whether you can actually accomplish all that you wish to do. As there are only twenty-four hours in a day, you must decide how best to use your time. With proper planning, you can make sound decisions.

Make a List

Figure 9.2 shows a list of Things to Do Today that might help Marquita organize her morning. Use it as inspiration for completing your own list in Control Builder 9.1: Things to Do Today (p. 116). Your list should include your daily activities from Control Builder 8.1: My Daily Log (p. 108). Sleeping, meals, exercise, leisure, and relaxation are essentials, although we often skip these whenever we need to make time for other tasks. Add any non-routine activities that may need to be done: paying utility bills, returning phone calls, making a dentist appointment.

FIGURE 9.2 Marquita's List

THINGS TO DO TODAY

Wake at 8:15
Shower/dress
Breakfast
Put out garbage
Prepare for interview
10:30 interview at Geodata, Inc.
Buy more envelopes and today's newspaper
Call Marshall re: interview on Friday
Balance checkbook
Go to Job Club for new listings
Write new cover letters
Mail résumés and cover letters
Make more copies of résumé
Pick up more milk and bread before dinnertime
Les over for dinner
Return library books due today
Do laundry

List Too Long?

If you've ended up with more tasks than you can possibly achieve in a day, don't feel overwhelmed. You can complete all these tasks—but not necessarily all on the same day. You need to transform this unwieldy, intimidating, and anxiety-provoking list into a simpler roster of tasks that you can achieve without losing control of your day.

List Too Short?

If your list is very short, don't think that you have nothing worthwhile to do. Recall your old routine. What did you do with your time before you began job hunting? What activities would you like to spend more time on? Review your goals from Control Builder 4.3: Goals I Want to Achieve (p. 48). What activities might help you achieve them?

Set Priorities

Regardless of the size of your list, the next step is to ask yourself these questions for each item you've listed.

- How important is this task in relation to my goal(s)?
- How long will this task take?
- Do I really have to do this task tomorrow?
- If I don't do this task tomorrow, when can I get it done?

Not everything you want to do is equally important. Start by identifying the most important thing you listed in Control Builder 9.1 and must do tomorrow. This first decision shapes how you use the rest of your time. Then go through your list and number your tasks in order of their importance.

What's Important?

Deciding what's important depends on several factors—your goals, deadlines, and resources. For example, if you've had health problems and your primary goal is to improve your health, going for a run may be more important that day than making extra copies of your résumé. Or if your phone bill must be paid by noon to prevent loss of service, then dealing with the phone company is your first priority. No hard-and-fast rules exist for prioritizing tasks on your list of Things to Do Today. Be flexible, and remember that each day is only a small part of a bigger picture.

How Long Will This Take?

Allowing a reasonable amount of time for each priority can

CONTROL 9.1 BUILDER

Things to Do Today

Date: ______________________

Morning

____

____

____

____

Afternoon

____

____

____

____

Evening

____

____

____

____

Notes

____

____

____

____

make all the difference between a realistic agenda or a blueprint for failure. Trying to cram thirty hours of activity into a twenty-four-hour day is guaranteed to increase your stress levels. If you had trouble prioritizing your list from Control Builder 9.1, Control Builder 9.2: What Can I Fit Into a Day? will help you determine whether you're planning your time sensibly.

CONTROL 9.2 BUILDER

What Can I Fit Into a Day?

(Use further sheets of paper as necessary.)

A. List of routine activities (e.g., breakfast — cooking, eating, cleaning up)	**Estimated time (hours)**
Total (A)	
B. List of errands (e.g., reviewing job ads)	**Estimated time (hours)**
Total (B)	
Grand Total (A + B)	

If your grand total is greater than 24 hours, remove or change some of the activities on your agenda.

Get Focused

If you find that you've listed more activities than you can comfortably fit into a twenty-four-hour day, then you have some decisions to make. Must you complete all these tasks on this particular day, or can you postpone or modify some of them?

If you don't have to complete a task on a specific day, don't give it a false sense of urgency. Consider leaving it for another day. Focus on the things that you must accomplish tomorrow.

Consider Logistics

A perfectly prioritized list of tasks that fit neatly into twenty-four hours will still fail if some of the tasks themselves are incompatible. An early-morning visit to the dentist, followed by a one-hour job interview, followed by a three-hour seminar in the afternoon may look like a feasible agenda. However, it becomes impractical when the dentist's waiting room turns out to be crowded, or if the seminar is out of town.

Don't fall into a logistics trap. Organize tasks according to when and how they need to be done. Avoid booking activities into every minute of the day. You'll need some leeway when things don't go as planned. Quick Tips: Master Important Tasks offers further suggestions on logistics.

Streamline Your Schedule

You haven't failed if Control Builder 9.2 shows that you can't get through all your tasks in one day. Indeed, you've just saved yourself the stress of attempting the impossible.

Figure 9.3 shows how Marquita might prioritize and pare down her list. Check your priorities from Control Builder 9.1 (p. 116). Can you eliminate or substitute tasks? Refine your own list into a realistic twenty-four-hour job-hunting day.

"But I Hate Making Lists"

Maybe so. But don't skip this step. Begin by making your list in your head. Set aside an uninterrupted block of time for this planning.

Once you have decided on the main things that you have to do tomorrow, slot these into your Daily Control Plan.

QUICK tips

Master Important Tasks

- Focus on one task at a time.
- Overestimate the time each task will take.
- Group tasks that can be done together. For example, all telephone calls or written work; errands within a few blocks of one another; consecutive appointments that allow traveling time.
- Spread out stress-provoking tasks. Don't try to tackle too many major decisions or deadlines on the same day.
- Break down big tasks into smaller ones that can be completed over several days.

THINGS TO DO TODAY

Wake at 8:15
Shower/dress
Breakfast
~~*Put out garbage*~~
Prepare for interview (**1)
10:30 interview at Geodata, Inc. (**2)
Buy more envelopes and today's newspaper
Call Marshall re: interview on Friday (**3)
~~*Balance checkbook*~~
~~*Go to Job Club for new listings*~~
Write new cover letters (**5)
Mail résumés and cover letters (**6)
Make more copies of résumé (**4)
~~*Pick up more milk and bread before dinnertime*~~
Les over for dinner
Return library books due today (**7)
~~*Do laundry*~~

FIGURE 9.3 Marquita's Prioritized and Streamlined List

Step 2: Prepare for Hassles

Look at your streamlined list of Things to Do Today. How many of the items are potentially stress-provoking hassles? (Check your Worst Stressors from Control Builder 5.1, p. 62.) Interviews, visits to the employment office, cold calls to companies regarding possible jobs can all produce stress reactions. If you know that these situations will be stress-provoking, don't just sit back passively waiting for them to happen. Prepare for them instead.

Don't Get Caught Off Guard

Nikita, a fashion consultant, got tired of being tongue-tied whenever she had to show her portfolio to interviewers. After reading a book on visualization exercises, she decided to rehearse for these stressful events.

> *"I started practicing a week before a big interview. At least once a day, I'd imagine myself walking into the waiting room, checking in with the receptionist, taking a seat, doing deep breathing exercises, then calmly walking into the interview room. I even prepared a little speech to introduce the various shots in my portfolio. I'd imagine the interviewers praising my work... Once my mental interview was over, I'd picture myself being offered the job. Then I'd stop rehearsing. I tried not to dwell on my anxiety... When I actually got an interview, the results were dramatic. I was still a little nervous in the waiting room. But I warmed up once I started giving my 'spiel.' After all, I'd done it so many times before."*

A mental rehearsal of a stress-provoking situation and your planned response can increase your sense of control and reduce the amount of stress you experience.

- Consider what might happen. What concerns you about the situation and your possible reaction?
- Plan a single strategy for handling the situation effectively.
- Go through the scenario mentally, acting out the events and your response.

It may be useful to rehearse in front of a mirror. Or ask a friend or relative to rehearse with you. Try various approaches until you find one that satisfies you. Then put your concerns out of your mind.

Record tomorrow's anticipated hassles, and your chosen strategy for dealing with each of them, on your Daily Control Plan.

Step 3: Don't Take Your Stress to Bed

Making sure you don't take your stress to bed with you is the last thing to do in preparing the night before. Sleep gives you an opportunity to escape the problems, obligations, and activities of your day. Ideally, it's eight or so hours of blissful repose—a chance to recharge your batteries so that you can face each day renewed.

When you take your problems to bed with you, either you lose sleep, or else the quality of your sleep suffers. You wake up feeling overwhelmed and hopeless. Instead of easing your stress with sleep, you carry over your stress from today to tomorrow. Your stress builds instead of returning to a manageable level.

Leave Problems Outside Your Bedroom Door

If you frequently lie awake worrying, have nightmares, or wake up in the middle of the night with your heart pounding, you need a break from stress.

Once you've completed your list of Things to Do for the next day, put it aside. Don't lie in bed, stewing over the upcoming hassles you may or may not experience. Instead, remind yourself of all the things that have gone well for you today. Quick Tips: Improve Your Sleep offers further practical suggestions.

Choose one strategy for ensuring a sound night's rest, and enter it into your Daily Control Plan.

QUICK tips

Improve Your Sleep

- Make your bedroom your sleeping room. Have a restful décor that's conducive to sleep.
- Have a relaxing bedtime ritual: listen to soothing music, read a favorite book (no horror stories!)—anything to signal your mind that it's time to unwind and go to sleep.
- Use the time before you go to sleep to congratulate yourself on what you have accomplished during the day, rather than replay the things that went wrong.
- Separate sleeping and working. If you must work in your bedroom, avoid working in bed. If you want to talk, think, or write about your problems, get out of bed.
- Keep a diary. Even if you don't write in it every day, occasionally jotting down troublesome thoughts and feelings can get them off your mind.
- If you don't enjoy writing, talk—to your partner, a friend (or a counseling line), even your reflection in the mirror. Just make sure you get out of bed before talking about the things that concern you.
- Do some vigorous activity during the daytime—you'll sleep better at night.

Remember: If your mornings are scrambled and hurried like Marquita's, learn to prepare the night before.

Have a Good Morning

It's noon, and Frank hits the snooze button on the clock radio yet again. It's getting harder and harder to get out of bed in the morning. Frank knows that staying up late is part of the problem. He dozes off. The alarm rings again. Frank remembers the job interview at 1:30. He also remembers his unfinished résumé. "Oh, what's the point?" he moans. He turns off the alarm, rolls over, and goes back to sleep. Not a wise decision, but Frank is too tired to care.

Unlike Marquita, Frank doesn't have mornings. He's caught in a vicious cycle of staying up too late and then oversleeping. As a result, he begins each day feeling lethargic, demoralized, and hopeless.

Sleep specialists recommend maintaining regular sleeping and waking times. Oversleeping disrupts your sleep pattern and creates a vicious cycle: you stay up later and wake exhausted in the morning. Although occasional oversleeping is not harmful, habitual oversleeping robs you of a valuable part of your day.

Don't Skip Mornings

Mornings set the tone of your day and affect the quality of your job search. Have a Good Morning involves four steps:

- Step 1: Get Out of Bed
- Step 2: Decide to Have a Good Day
- Step 3: Give Yourself a Treat
- Step 4: Allow Yourself Extra Time.

Step 1: Get Out of Bed

Begin each day by giving yourself a reason to get out of bed at a suitable time. Fight those excuses to oversleep.

Choose a waking time that fits with your natural sleep pattern—and stick to it. Quick Tips: Get Out of Bed! lists some helpful strategies. Find one that works for you.

Why Are You Oversleeping?

Oversleeping is not necessarily a sign of laziness. It may be the result of a bad habit, such as staying up late. Or there may be a physical reason, such as the onset of a cold or flu. Lethargy and oversleeping can also be symptoms of emotional distress or depression.

QUICK tips

Get Out of Bed!

Avoid the snooze button—get up when the alarm goes off. And have 3 reasons for getting out of bed already prepared. Here are some suggestions:

- Make breakfast for your family
- Do a morning work-out with a TV program
- Have someone give you a wake-up call
- Meet a friend for breakfast or a game of squash
- Walk the dog
- Go to the corner store to buy a newspaper
- Enroll in a group or class that meets in the morning
- Tune in to a morning talk show
- Plan to work in the library, and be there for opening time
- Sleep with the blinds or curtains open so that the sunlight wakes you
- Roll out of bed onto the floor and do gentle calisthenics or stretching
- Put the clock radio on the other side of the room
- Give yourself a reward as soon as you get out of bed.

Fit the Solution to the Problem

Different problems require different solutions. Understanding what keeps you in bed helps you develop a strategy for tackling the problem directly. Sergio's and Soo-Yin's experiences illustrate the importance of selecting a remedy that matches the problem.

Sergio, a laid-off truck driver, doesn't understand why he's oversleeping. He goes to bed early even though he naps during the day. Once up, he has little energy, and his appetite is poor. He spends hours in front of the TV. Sergio feels hopeless about his situation. He has tried many tricks for getting out of bed in the morning: putting the alarm clock on the other side of the room, opening the curtains—nothing works.

Sergio may be depressed in response to his recent job loss. A good starting point for him might be a visit to a health care practitioner who is familiar with his physical and mental health profiles. Sergio may benefit from therapeutic interventions to deal with depression, such as private counseling, attending a support group, beginning an aerobics exercise program, or medication.

Soo-Yin has spent a lot of time at home since she lost her job as a hospital administrator. At first, she got up at the same time she did when she was working. She began each day eager to continue her job search. Now, four months later, Soo-Yin is discouraged by her lack of results. She knows she'll feel more energetic and accomplish more if she gets out of bed. But getting up in the morning seems pointless.

In Soo-Yin's case, concrete activities that give her a sense of purpose may be useful. Making breakfast for a friend, meeting with a networking group, or getting to the library by a certain time are all strategies that could give her the boost she needs.

The possibilities are endless. All begin with understanding what keeps you in bed. If getting up in the morning is a problem for you, Control Builder 9.3: What Keeps Me In Bed? (p. 124) can assist you.

Decide on a reasonable time for waking up tomorrow, and write it into your Daily Control Plan. (If necessary, include one hint from from Quick Tips: Get Out of Bed!)

CONTROL 9.3 BUILDER

What Keeps Me in Bed?

What Happens Now

What I Can Change

In the morning...

- What do I do?
- What do I say to myself?
- How do I feel?

The first step I am going to take to get myself out of bed in the morning is to

____

____

____

Step 2: Decide to Have a Good Day

It's gray outside when John, an actor, wakes up. "Oh, it looks miserable outside. I hope it isn't going to be one of those days," he mumbles. Then he looks in the mirror, surveying his graying hair and the bags under his eyes. "I don't look too good today. Oh well, what do you expect; it's one of those days." While John is making breakfast, the juice jug crashes to the floor. "Great!" he exclaims, "I knew something like that would happen. Here we go again." Throughout the day, he waits for something else to go awry.

Often we decide the kind of day that we're going to have without even realizing that we've made a decision. Then we interpret the rest of the day based on that decision.

When you talk to yourself in the way that John does, you have decided to have a bad day. Consequently, your response to all events tends to be negative. Eventually, you do have a bad day.

Make Every Day a Good Day

You can select any day on the calendar, circle it in red ink, decide that it will be a good day, and then go on to have a good day.

Deciding to have a good day won't guarantee that negative events won't occur. But it will shape your response to these events. Your response to negative events doesn't have to be negative.

You Deserve Good Days

To have good days, you also need to believe that you deserve them. Don't convince yourself that good days happen only to others—not you.

We have many different ways of telling ourselves that we don't deserve good days. The "Thank Goodness It's Friday" mentality is one. You spend the entire week waiting for Fridays and the weekend. You dread Mondays because they are miserable. And you believe that from Tuesday to Thursday the days become progressively worse. This thinking allows you to have only two good days per week. Five-sevenths of a lifetime is a lot of time to spend having bad days when you can decide to make every day a good day.

The next time you notice yourself about to say, "It's going to be one of those days," hold your tongue or change your thought. Begin each day by deciding that you're going to have a good day. Then make it a good one.

As you fill in your Daily Control Plan, write yourself a reminder to have a good day tomorrow. Put this reminder in a place where you will see it as soon as you get up in the morning.

Step 3: Give Yourself a Treat

Just thinking positive thoughts isn't enough. Do something nice for yourself. Your morning treat doesn't have to be lavish or time-consuming. It can be as simple as savoring a cup of your favorite herbal tea, going for a walk, listening to music you enjoy, or having some quiet time alone.

Pampering yourself in the morning gives your self-esteem a boost. Knowing that a treat awaits you gives you something to look forward to as you get out of bed. Your morning treat also reinforces the idea that the day is going to be a good one: after all, one good thing has already happened to you! Indulging yourself a bit makes mornings seem less inhospitable, even to avowed non-"morning persons." Take advantage of this early opportunity to feel good.

Short on ideas for morning treats? Remind yourself of the things you enjoy doing at other times of the day. Then complete Control Builder 9.4: My Morning Treat (p. 126).

CONTROL 9.4 BUILDER

My Morning Treat

Things I like to do during the day or evening

____

____

How can I fit these into the morning?

____

____

A treat for every day of the week (fill in one for each day):

Monday _______________________________________

Tuesday _______________________________________

Wednesday _____________________________________

Thursday ______________________________________

Friday ____

Saturday ______________________________________

Sunday ____

Write tomorrow's morning treat into your Daily Control Plan.

Step 4: Allow Yourself Extra Time

The benefits of a good morning can quickly disappear if you run around frantically trying to get through your list of Things to Do Today. Disorganized and hectic mornings leave you feeling frazzled and out of control for the rest of the day.

Give Yourself Leeway

To avoid having rushed, scrambled mornings, make sure you have enough time to complete the tasks you want to do. Then give yourself leeway in case something goes wrong or takes longer than you anticipated. You don't necessarily have to wake up earlier than usual. Instead, you might plan to do less in the morning; or you could reorganize your morning routine to suit the amount of time you have after waking. You might also gradually increase the amount of usable time in your morning by "finding" a few minutes every day.

- Write your morning activities into your Daily Control Plan from the time you wake up until you leave the house. (If you're not planning to go out, make 10:00 or 10:30 the end of your morning.)
- Estimate the amount of time each of these activities will take. If you cannot realistically expect to accomplish all these activities, discard some of the least important, or consider getting an earlier start.

Be Ready to Face Your Day

How would the steps of Have a Good Morning change things for Marquita and Frank?

> *Marquita wakes before the alarm goes off and rolls out of bed feeling rested. Sleepless nights are a thing of the past. The phone rings as she heads for the shower—it's Geodata, the company Marquita called yesterday, confirming her 10:30 interview for today. Marquita continues with her morning routine. There are still one and a half hours to dress, exercise, and have breakfast before catching the 8:30 bus. After breakfast, Marquita consults her streamlined list of Things to Do Today. "Interview at 10:30; remember notes on dining room table," it says. Marquita picks up her notes on the way out and walks to the bus stop.*

Over at Frank's place:

> *It's 9:30 and as the alarm goes off, Frank automatically reaches for the snooze button—then remembers that the clock is now on the other side of the room. He stumbles out of bed, turns on the light and the radio. Bright light and music fill the room. Frank goes into the kitchen and puts on water for café au lait—a special treat. He notices his finished résumé on the table and remembers that he has an interview today. He also has a telephone meeting beforehand with a friend so that he can rehearse. "I hate mornings," Frank mumbles, then stops and corrects himself. "I'm going to make the most of that interview today."*

You too can change your mornings. You can be more relaxed, better organized, and ready to face your day. You don't have to have frantic, disorganized mornings—or no mornings at all.

What's Next?

Your day doesn't end at 11:00 a.m. So move on to Chapter 10: Hang In There for strategies to make your job-hunting day more productive and satisfying.

REMEMBER

- ✔ The night before, make a prioritized list of Things to Do.
- ✔ Before going to bed, let yourself unwind and put your troubles aside. You'll sleep better and get a break from your stress.
- ✔ Habitual oversleeping robs you of a valuable part of your day. Explore why you oversleep, and find ways to get out of bed in the morning.
- ✔ Decide to have a good day—and make your day a good one.
- ✔ Avoid scrambled mornings. Give yourself extra time to get through your morning routine.
- ✔ Modify your Daily Control Plan to suit any day's commitments.

CHAPTER 10

Hang In There

You've made it through the morning. Now the day looms ahead of you. What happens next? Do you feel as though you are running through a minefield—scrambling to avoid disaster, being hit by unexpected problems, never feeling certain that you'll make it to the end of the day? Or do you spend your afternoons watching the hours drag by, not knowing how to fill the time?

You don't have to struggle through each day. With the Daily Control Plan, you can learn to Hang In There.

FIGURE 10.1 The Daily Control Plan

How can you take control of your days, yet "go with the flow"? Paradoxically, the first step in increasing your control is to recognize that you cannot control everything that happens. Figure 10.2 lists some of the things you can and cannot control.

You Can't Control Everything

You're not admitting defeat by acknowledging that some things are beyond your control. Trying to control *all* your daily events can make you frantic and harried. Overwhelmed by the constant struggle, you are likely to give up. Distinguishing between what you can and cannot control enables you to stop blaming yourself and to take credit for what you have achieved.

You Can Control Your Own	You Cannot Control Other People's
• Thoughts • Feelings • Responses • Decisions • Actions • Stress levels	• Feelings • Responses • Decisions • Actions

Figure 10.2 How Much Can You Control?

Put your energy to good use by concentrating on what you *can* control.

Have a Two-Goal Day

You can control your thoughts and actions. You can also control your stress levels—especially if you start each day by reminding yourself of two goals:

- To make it to the end of the day without giving up on the Daily Control Plan
- To keep your stress at a manageable level.

In the short run, these two goals are the most important ones for you to achieve each day. To achieve them, you may need to set aside some other goals and expectations that would otherwise cause you undue pressure. These include trying to eliminate all stress, get through all the items on your list of Things to Do, follow your Stress Control Plan to the letter, or avoid all conflict.

The next stage of the Daily Control Plan—Hang In There—shows you how to achieve your daily goals by structuring and pacing your days. Hang In There breaks down into six smaller steps:

- Step 1: Get Out of the House
- Step 2: Take Things As They Come
- Step 3: Get Support
- Step 4: Monitor Your Stress Levels
- Step 5: Pause to Relax
- Step 6: Keep Your Thoughts Positive.

At Home—In the Doldrums

In Chapter 9, you saw how Frank's day begins. How does that day unfold?

Days drag by for Frank. There isn't much to do around the apartment, but he doesn't have the energy to go out. Today's agenda is pretty much like yesterday's: watch TV, have a nap, read a novel, eat a snack, complete his résumé. The résumé has been sitting, unfinished, on the kitchen table for days. Frank spends yet another day wandering around his apartment, becoming more and more restless.

Frank has become apathetic and defeated. Staying at home has long ago ceased to be relaxing. Now, it is a problem.

Staying at home is not taboo. However, like regular oversleeping, habitually spending your days indoors is detrimental to your job search.

Staying home on a regular basis can

- Encourage physical inactivity and lethargy
- Reinforce your feelings of non-productivity
- Isolate you from people who might bolster your job search
- Increase feelings of depression and hopelessness
- Erode your motivation and self-image.

Give yourself a fighting chance. Resist becoming trapped in your home.

Step 1: Get Out of the House

Where Can I Go?

Anywhere. Initially, where you go and what you do are less important than the fact that you are getting out. Take the kids to school; meet a friend for lunch, conversation, and mutual support; have a swim at the neighborhood "Y." Unless you have a reason to be at home, try to get out of the house, preferably early in the day.

If you must spend your morning at home, then schedule some time out of the house during the afternoon. This can help you break out of the energy slump that often results from staying at home all day.

Take It Slow

When you've been feeling depressed and lethargic, leaving the house may take great effort. If you balk at the idea of going out, then take it slow: getting out even two afternoons out of five is better than staying in all week. Make your excursions pleasurable adventures—and keep reminding yourself of all the benefits of getting out.

Getting out of the house can

- Lift your spirits
- Energize you
- Restore your sense of purpose
- Make you feel productive
- Give you the get-up-and-go to tackle your job-search tasks.

Don't overplan your first trips out. Just select your destination. Once you're out, you'll find it easier to get on with the rest of your day of job hunting.

Before you talk yourself into staying indoors tomorrow, put pen to paper in Control Builder 10.1 (p. 132) and plan places you can go.

CONTROL 10.1 BUILDER

Where Can I Go?

1. Places within walking distance of my home:

____

____

____

2. Places I can go by car or public transportation:

____

____

____

3. Places I can go alone:

____

____

____

4. Places where I can meet people:

____

____

____

5. Places where I can get work done:

____

____

____

6. Places where I can unwind:

____

____

____

Mark the time you will leave home tomorrow on your Daily Control Plan, and specify your destination.

If you haven't been out in a few days, don't be overly concerned with what you will do. Once you're out, stay out for at least an hour.

Step 2: Take Things As They Come

What do you do once you're out of the house? The way our friend Marquita passes her day is a study in nerve-wracking, debilitating chaos.

For Marquita, the roller coaster ride continues. She dashes from place to place without making any progress with her list of Things to Do Today. Little things go wrong. Tasks are forgotten. Marquita gets side-tracked on a few small errands and is late for an important appointment. In the ensuing scramble, she doesn't have enough time to eat. By 5:00, she is exhausted and irritable.

Get Off the Roller Coaster

As usual, Marquita is frantic and disorganized. Each day of her job search is a struggle to stay in control. Marquita needs to get off this endless roller coaster ride. If your days are like hers, then so do you.

During your day, you encounter many stress-provoking situations. Some are predictable, while some seem to arise out of the blue. Don't try to anticipate and control every event that occurs. Instead, prepare when you know that a stressor is approaching. And for those occasions that you can't anticipate, make a decision to roll with the punches.

Be Prepared

Review your Worst Stressors from Control Builder 5.1 (p. 62). If you completed a Stress Control Plan Worksheet (Control Builder 6.2, pp. 80–81) for any of these, you have already drawn up a plan for dealing with some situations. Being prepared puts you one step ahead of the game. When a stressor arises, you have a plan in hand to deal with it.

Enter any anticipated stressors for tomorrow, and your strategy for dealing with each, into your Daily Control Plan.

"Help! My Plan Failed"

Things don't always go as you plan. Situations for which you cannot prepare require a different approach.

How do you usually deal with stressors that you could not foresee, or situations in which your Stress Control Plan does not apply? Do you overreact quickly? Knee-jerk responses actually increase your stress levels. And often, the decisions that you make under pressure create further problems.

The Five-Step Crisis Buster

The next time an unexpected challenge arises, try something different: do nothing!

Unless you are in a life-threatening situation that requires immediate action, try this Five-Step Crisis Buster:

1. Stop
2. Force yourself to take a few deep breaths
3. Think about the situation
4. Check out your self-talk and counter any negative statements
5. Try to come up with an appropriate solution.

Act on your plan only after you've completed all these steps.

You may find that an apparent lack of immediate response makes some people around you uncomfortable. So be it. Don't let yourself be pressured into taking hasty action. Following a calmer course can dramatically lower your stress levels.

Roll with the Punches

When it seems as though problems are coming at you from all directions, don't panic. Whether you have too much or too little to do during the day, learn to roll with the punches. Being flexible helps you stay in control. Sticking rigidly to plans that you've made only adds to your frustration and stress.

Step 3: Get Support

> *"Now it seems funny, but at the time I was frantic," recalls Bernice, an occupational therapist. "I left home without bringing the address and phone number for my interview. I stood in the subway station, debating whether I could make it home and back in time. Then I realized that my roommate Tasha, who works just a block away from our apartment, could help. All it took was two phone calls. Within fifteen minutes, she was able to give me the address, phone number, and some pointers for the interview that hadn't occurred to me. She was a lifesaver."*

As you grapple with the expected and unexpected events that arise during the day, remember that you don't have to deal with them alone. Whether you're feeling overwhelmed by the demands and frantic pace of your day, or by depression and lethargy, reach out. Be open to assistance from others.

Find ways of lightening your burden with the help of the people in your life. Express your feelings; ask for help or information; share a break. Accept help and encouragment from those around you.

Chapter 14: Have Someone On Your Side explores practical strategies for developing supportive relationships during your job search.

If tomorrow's Daily Control Plan contains a task that is particularly difficult, consider who might give you support for accomplishing it, and how they might help. Make a note on your Plan to contact them.

Step 4: Monitor Your Stress Levels

Despite your best intentions, you may still find yourself getting stressed during the day. This is not a sign of failure. Your goal isn't to eliminate *all* stress. Your goal is to keep your stress at a manageable level.

As your day progresses, pause occasionally to monitor how much stress you are experiencing. Here are some simple ways to track your stress levels.

Three-Point Stress Check

Stop and assess yourself for these three common signs of tension:

- **Check your breathing.** Is it shallow and fast, or are you holding your breath?
- **Check your shoulders.** Where are they—inching up towards your ears? Are your shoulder and neck muscles tense?
- **Check your thoughts.** Are you putting yourself down, exaggerating the situation, being illogical?

Your Stress Barometer

Since everyone responds to stress differently, sometimes a spot check isn't enough. Review Quick Tips: My Stress Barometer (p. 64) to keep track of how much pressure you're under.

Reminders

It takes time to learn to recognize your signs of stress and to remember to check your stress levels throughout the day. As you acquire these positive habits, keep encouraging yourself to relax. Just as an actor learns a new role, you can cue yourself to monitor your stress:

- Set the alarm on your watch. Whenever it rings, quickly check your state of body and mind.
- Leave yourself cue cards with reminders and encouraging messages.
- Stick brightly colored adhesive dots in places where you tend to get stressed—for example, over your desk. Each time you see the dot, take a moment to take a few deep breaths.

Whatever works for *you* is a good cue.

Choose at least one method for checking your stress levels tomorrow. Select three times during the day when you might pause to check your stress, and enter them into your Daily Control Plan.

Step 5: Pause to Relax

It's obvious that Marquita needs to relax. But relaxation would also benefit Frank, even though he seems to do nothing but laze around at home.

Using a structured relaxation technique, like those described in Chapter 7, is one of the best ways to get off the roller coaster or out of the doldrums. Taking a relaxation break during your day will energize you, clear your thoughts, and allow you to change the pace of your day. If you're going at breakneck speed, you can slow down. If you've been lethargic, a relaxation pick-me-up can help you get back on track. Then you can review your list of Things to Do Today, reprioritize, and reorganize.

Don't Wait for the End of the Day

At least once before the end of the day, take a ten- to twenty-minute relaxation break. Don't be afraid to take this time. You won't "lose steam," and your day won't fall apart. On the contrary—you'll pick up energy. And don't wait until your day is nearly over. By then, your stresses will have accumulated and you will find it harder to unwind.

If you're tempted to skip your relaxation break, try one of the instant techniques in Quick Tips: Sure-Fire Stress Busters.

On your Daily Control Plan, block out a twenty-five-minute period specifically for relaxation. If you cannot fit in a full relaxation break, select one of the Sure-Fire Stress Busters instead.

QUICK tips

Sure-Fire Stress Busters

- Sit still and close your eyes. Picture yourself somewhere pleasant (the beach, hiking in the mountains). Spend a few minutes there before coming back to the hustle and bustle of your day.
- Gently massage your temples and scalp with your fingertips.
- Sit in a comfortable position. Take a few slow, deep breaths. Then close your eyes and picture the path that the air takes as it enters your nose and leaves your mouth. Slowly open your eyes. Keep your breathing slow for a few minutes.
- Raise your shoulders up to your ears. Hold, counting to ten. Let shoulders drop. Roll shoulders back five times, then forward five times.
- Stand up and have a good stretch. (Two or three are even better.) Inhale deeply; exhale, with a sigh at the end of each stretch.
- To loosen up your hands and feet, squeeze hands into tight fists and hold for a count of five; relax. Repeat two or three times. Shake hands out. Curl toes and arch feet to tighten muscles; then make circles with toes to loosen.
- Failed the Three-Point Stress Check? Take a slow, deep breath in; exhale, sighing, through your mouth. Slowly lower your shoulders and feel the tension leaving your muscles. Switch negative thoughts with positive statements. Or simply concentrate on something else: mentally recite a poem or the lyrics to your favorite song—anything to switch off that negative chatter.

Step 6: Think Positively

"It was too good to be true. I was zipping through my job-search tasks. I should have known that my luck couldn't last," says Roy, a graphic designer. "I backed my wheelchair over the cord for my computer and accidentally unplugged it. And poof—my whole résumé disappeared! I was so caught up in composing it that I hadn't saved my file. Three hours of work down the drain! So much for having a good day."

It takes more than your initial decision to have a good day to make that day a good one. Having a good day requires effort.

Don't become negative the moment you hit a snag. Instead:

- Talk back to your inner critic, using the techniques from Chapter 3
- See if you can reinterpret the situation and find something positive in it.

If you can't find any redeeming qualities in the situation, don't let it ruin your day. Put the event out of your mind and get on with your "good" day—even when it seems as though everything that could possibly go wrong has. Remind yourself that you can take problems in stride.

Positive interpretations lead to positive responses, even in difficult situations. Get into the habit of thinking positively. Eventually, positive thinking will carry you through even the most difficult days.

Choose two positive statements to help you overcome your inner critic, and enter these into your Daily Control Plan.

Sail Through Your Day

If Frank and Marquita were to try the Daily Control Plan, you can be sure their days would be different.

As Frank steps out into the sunshine, he wonders how he could have stayed in his apartment day after day. "Never mind," he thinks. "I'm past that now." And indeed, he is. Today's agenda:

- *Breakfast with Patricia (practice for interview)*
- *Interview at 11:00*
- *Home to do T'ai Chi and have lunch*
- *To employment office to check job listings.*

Perhaps he might go to the movies with his sister tonight—it's half-price night. Frank smiles and strides along with the crowd.

It's 9:50. The bus is inching its way through morning traffic. Marquita resists the urge to look at her watch. She knows it will only make her more anxious about being late for her 10:30 interview at Geodata. She checks her shoulders—sure enough, they're up around her ears. Marquita lets them drop. Her breathing? Yes, she's been holding her breath again. Then Marquita wrestles her panicky thoughts into submission. "I am calm," she reassures herself. "Worrying won't make the bus go any faster." She glances at her list of Things to Do Today and mentally crosses out the errand she was going to do before her interview—she'll make time for it tomorrow. Finally, Marquita pulls out her notes and buckles down to the job of psyching herself up for her interview.

Days like these are a vast improvement over languishing in the doldrums or riding an endless roller coaster of anxiety. Don't fight your way through each afternoon of your job search. Hang In There instead.

What's Next?

With your day of job hunting behind you, you're coming into the home stretch. Turn to Chapter 11 for tips on how to Go for a Strong Finish, and make your evenings as rewarding as your days.

- ✔ Learn which events are within your control and concentrate on tackling these.
- ✔ Get out of the house each day. Habitually staying at home can be detrimental to your job search.
- ✔ Use cues or reminders to keep track of your stress levels throughout the day. Pause to relax whenever your stress levels rise.
- ✔ Prepare for stressors that you can predict, and roll with the punches when something unexpected occurs. Your Stress Control Plan can help you stay cool and collected in a crisis.
- ✔ Ask for, and accept, support from the people in your life.
- ✔ Don't let negative events ruin your "good" day. Keep your thoughts positive.

CHAPTER 11

Go for a Strong Finish

At last the day is over. Now you can collapse on the sofa and forget the ups and downs of your day—right? Wrong!

You've got the whole evening ahead of you. It's time to Go for a Strong Finish. You can catch your second wind and have evenings every bit as full and pleasurable as your days.

How do Marquita and Frank wrap up their job-hunting day? Not surprisingly, Marquita fizzles when she runs out of steam.

Marquita slumps on the sofa, exhausted after a hectic day. "Thank goodness that's over," she sighs. She turns on the TV and switches rapidly from channel to channel: her racing thoughts make it impossible to concentrate. She gives up and goes into the kitchen to get dinner. A cold beer is first on the menu. Beer in hand, Marquita surveys the contents of the fridge but can't decide on dinner. Exasperated, she grabs some leftover macaroni and cheese and tosses it into the microwave. Marquita paces impatiently while her meal heats. Dinner in hand, she returns to the living room and plops down in front of the TV. An hour later, Marquita is asleep on the sofa.

Frank's evening is not much better.

Frank looks at the clock again: it's 8:30 p.m. What now? After a day of continuous snacking, dinner seems pointless. Three hours to fill before the late-night talk shows begin. Frank wanders aimlessly from room to room. He isn't tired—he had a nap earlier—but somehow he still doesn't have the energy to work on his résumé. "What's the point?" Frank sighs. He feels as though the room is closing in around him. And it's only 8:35.

Having dreary, unproductive evenings is a bad habit. And like any other bad habit, it can be changed. The final stage of the Daily Control Plan—Go for a Strong Finish—breaks down into four smaller steps:

- Step 1: Punch the Clock
- Step 2: Reward Yourself
- Step 3: Put the Day Behind You
- Step 4: Let Yourself Unwind.

Step 1: Punch the Clock

Your Day Is Like a Marathon

Long-distance marathon runners are good role models. No matter how gruelling the run, no matter how much they've slowed down or how exhausted they are, they always try to go for a strong finish. Inspired by the sight of the finish line, they give it their all. This strategy pays off at the Olympics, so why not put it to work to improve your evenings?

FIGURE 11.1 The Daily Control Plan

Where Is Your Finish Line?

"After years of putting in fifteen-hour days as a corporate lawyer, I didn't know how to turn myself off at the end of a day," confesses Amarjit. "When I started looking for a new job, I stuck with my old habits: I worked until I was too tired to continue, then went straight to bed. If there wasn't anything left to do and I'd planned my next week's job-search strategy, I'd end up getting irritable and climbing the walls because I didn't know what to do with myself. A few weeks of this pace convinced me that I needed to change my evening routine."

Before you can Go for a Strong Finish, you must have a finish line in sight.

If you do not currently have a regular job, you may lack the usual cues that signal the end of the day, such as clearing your desk, putting your tools away, punching the clock, or traveling home in rush hour. You need to replace these familiar end-of-day cues by setting yourself a suitable time to "punch the clock."

Respect Your Work Day

Right now, your job-hunting day is your work day. Like any other work day, it needs to have a beginning and an end.

Try to get your job-search tasks done by your designated quitting time. If some tasks are left uncompleted, plan to finish them tomorrow. Avoid habitually working overtime. You may think that you're getting more done by working late, but eventually this habit leads to burnout and inefficiency. As well, decide when you are going to end your evening, and stick to this schedule.

Control Builder 11.1 (p. 142) will help you set your finish line and get more out of your evening.

Enter the times for ending your work day and for going to bed on your Daily Control Plan.

Catch Your Second Wind

If you enjoy running or some other strenuous physical activity, then you know the phenomenon of catching your second wind. You reach a point where you feel exhausted and unable to continue. Yet, if you will yourself to go on, you tap a new surge of energy. Then you feel as though you could go on forever.

Similarly, if you stop at that first wave of fatigue which most job hunters experience at the end of a day, you won't have a chance to catch your second wind.

When your designated quitting time arrives, tell yourself: "This is the beginning of a great evening." The steps that follow will ensure that your evening is indeed a good one.

Step 2: Reward Yourself

What better way to start a pleasant evening than with a treat? This is not self-indulgence. Rather, it's a reward.

You Deserve It!

First, remind yourself of all the things that went well during your day. Don't replay the things that went wrong. Then, reward yourself by doing something that you really enjoy.

Rewards don't have to be elaborate, expensive, or time-consuming. Similar to your morning treat, your evening reward can be any activity that you enjoy: an invigorating foam bath, a cup of gourmet decaffeinated coffee, listening to music. It's your choice.

CONTROL 11.1 BUILDER

My Finish Line

- Decide when your job-hunting work day ends and when your evening begins.

  I will punch the clock at ______________________

- Mark your evening finish line: your bedtime.

  I will go to bed at ______________________

Don't Skip Rewards

Pierre, an unemployed X-ray technician, balks at the idea of giving himself rewards. "Why celebrate if I haven't landed a job?" is his way of thinking.

While this habit of mind is difficult to change, Pierre might compromise by setting himself daily quotas for his job-search tasks, each with its own reward. For example, if he succeeds in mailing five résumés, he might reward himself with half an hour's swim at the "Y."

Rewards are important. They help you feel good about the changes you are trying to make in your life. They also give you something to look forward to as you Hang In There during the day. It's a lot easier to make it through your two o'clock slump when you know that there's a treat in store for you later.

Before your resolve to be good to yourself wavers, take the time to plan your evening reward with Control Builder 11.2 (p. 144). Be sure to keep your rewards positive. You don't want to choose rewards that will cause you further problems in the long run, such as overeating, or relying on alcohol or drugs to unwind.

Once you've chosen tomorrow's evening reward, enter it on your Daily Control Plan.

Step 3: Put the Day Behind You

Linda, an ESL teacher, just can't lay her botched interview to rest: "When she told me that my experience teaching high school was no preparation for handling an adult class, I should have remembered the list of my transferable skills that I drew up yesterday. I can't believe I used that corny 'I'm willing to learn anything' line instead. When will I learn to say the right thing at interviews?"

You can't get on with your evening until you put the day behind you. Once your official quitting time arrives, stop replaying your day.

Every time you begin to think about something that went wrong, say "stop" mentally. Train yourself to switch thoughts whenever you start to replay your day. Make a list of all the good things that happened. Congratulate yourself for what you feel you did well or tried to do differently.

Then, stop analyzing your day. If you find it hard to switch off the day's events, find a diversion. Select a leisure activity that will occupy your mind: computer games, Scrabble, house

CONTROL 11.2 BUILDER

My Evening Reward

Things I like to do during the day:

____

____

How can I fit these into the evening?

____

____

A treat for every night of the week (fill in one for each evening):

Monday ______________________________

Tuesday ______________________________

Wednesday ______________________________

Thursday ______________________________

Friday ______________________________

Saturday ______________________________

Sunday ______________________________

plants, drawing. Or work off tension by engaging in a physical activity such as jogging, cycling, or house cleaning.

Avoid conversations with people who like to talk about negative things. If you still feel a need to complain, try Quick Tips: Need to Complain? to put a period to your day.

Step 4: Let Yourself Unwind

Ideally, you should have one or two hours free between your quitting time and the time at which you plan your next day. If this isn't the case, then remove one or two earlier activities from your Daily Control Plan.

On your Plan, circle at least one half hour for leisure. Enjoy a book, take a walk, call a friend, visit with family, do relaxation exercises—what you do is less important than the fact that you're doing it.

QUICK tips

Need to Complain?

Have a formal "worry and complain" session at the end of your day.

- Set the alarm on your watch or clock for five minutes.
- During these five minutes, replay all the things that went wrong today. Feel free to vent your feelings about how bad you feel. Be as miserable as you like.
- Stop when the alarm goes off.
- If you still have things that you want to worry or complain about, save them for the next evening's session.

"But I Don't Have Time to Unwind!"

> *"Unwind in the evening? That'll be the day!" muses Mario, a single parent who juggles his job search with part-time clerical work and the demands of raising three children. "Once I step in the front door, no one even cares what kind of day I had. I've got three hungry kids to feed, homework to supervise, and a house to clean. And this is the only time I have to prepare cover letters and résumés. I can't even remember if I have a hobby, let alone take time to enjoy it."*

If your household obligations don't permit you much time for yourself in the evening, squeeze in your leisure time before you return home: a quick workout at the gym, a late afternoon movie, or half an hour browsing through the public library.

Make it clear to your loved ones that you need a certain amount of time for yourself at the end of your day. Stick to your guns, even if there is an uproar. Enjoy at least half an hour of leisure time every day. You deserve it.

Prepare for Sleep

How you spend your evening also affects the quality of your sleep. For restful sleep, you need to let go of the day's tensions before you get into bed.

Many people believe that they naturally unwind when they go to sleep. This isn't the case. Sleeping and relaxing are not the same. People who have stressful days are often too tense to sleep well—unless they take time to unwind first.

Avoid Sleep Disturbers

Quick Tips: Improve Your Sleep (p. 121) suggested some techniques to use just before going to bed. As well, here are some common pitfalls to avoid:

- Drinking coffee, hot chocolate, caffeinated soft drinks, or alcohol may soothe you in the short term but will keep you awake at night. (This is also true of smoking cigarettes.)
- Heavy meals, or those containing stimulants such as sugar and chocolate, should not be eaten close to bedtime.
- What you read, watch, or listen to before bed can adversely affect your sleep. The news, murder mysteries, and loud music can overstimulate you and make it difficult to fall asleep.
- Replaying negative events can not only keep you awake; it can also cause bad dreams.
- Anxiety-provoking or highly emotional situations hamper your sleep.
- Strenuous physical activity close to bedtime can leave you too energized to sleep well.
- Relaxation exercises just prior to sleeping can also be energizing. Relaxation at bedtime is advisable only for people who have such high levels of tension that they cannot otherwise unwind enough to fall asleep.

Still Can't Sleep?

If you've tried all these hints and still have difficulty sleeping, monitor what you do for a few hours before you retire. Control Builder 11.3 can help you identify and eliminate possible sleep disturbers.

Don't Stop Yet

Now the cycle for your day of job hunting is complete. It's time to begin night-before preparations for tomorrow's job-search agenda, as described in Chapter 9.

As you finish sketching your plans for tomorrow, include a time for planning the day after tomorrow (half an hour will do). Mark this on your Daily Control Plan.

What's Next?

You've seen how the Daily Control Plan can make each day of your job search more productive, relaxed, and enjoyable. Now turn to Chapter 12 to learn how to extend the Daily Control Plan to prepare for a week, a month, or longer.

CONTROL 11.3 BUILDER

Eliminate Sleep Disturbers

Monitor yourself for two to three days in a row to identify these potential sleep disturbers. Check (✔) any that seem to apply to you.

Sleep Disturbers	**Day 1**	**Day 2**	**Day 3**
Stimulants—food and drink • No. cups coffee, tea, hot chocolate, caffeinated soft drinks • No. alcoholic beverages • No. candy bars, junk foods, desserts • No. cigarettes smoked			
Emotional situations?			
Heavy evening meals?			
Stress-provoking situations?			
Strenuous exercise?			
Other stimulating activities that may interfere with my sleep (specify):			

If you find that your sleeplessness continues, ask your health care practitioner for a referral to a Sleep Disorders Clinic. The Bibliography on page 210 includes a book on this subject.

REMEMBER

- ✔ Set yourself a regular quitting time and stick to it.
- ✔ Begin each evening with a reward for your day's job-search efforts.
- ✔ Take time to unwind before you get into bed at night.
- ✔ Improve the quality of your sleep by identifying and eliminating sleep-disturbing activities.

CHAPTER 12

Plan Ahead

Once you've mastered daily planning, broaden your horizons by planning farther in advance. You can plan for weeks, months, or years.

Planning ahead doesn't commit you to carrying out all your specified activities. It does give you a clearer picture of where you are headed over time.

Naturally, a Weekly (or Monthly or Yearly) Control Plan won't contain the detail of your daily schedule. Nor does it mean you can discard your Daily Control Plan.

Benefits of the Big Picture

Longer-term schedules have several advantages. They

- Encourage you to keep multiple objectives and deadlines in sight
- Help you to prioritize the tasks on your Daily Control Plans
- Enable you to organize your goals and chart your progress toward attaining them
- Show you how each day fits into your overall plan of action for your job search and beyond.

Your Week at a Glance

Use the same steps from your Daily Control Plan to schedule a week, a month, or a year. The rule of thumb is to use less detail when planning for a longer period. Also:

- Begin with a blank calendar in front of you.
- Arrange your routine activities into general categories—for example, Job-Search Tasks, Leisure Time, Self-Improvement.
- Try to project your upcoming deadlines and important milestones. This is where your earlier goals come in (Control Builder 4.3: Goals I Want to Achieve, p. 48).
- Note the date by which you hope to complete each goal, as well as deadlines for each smaller step on the way to it. How many goals and deadlines you include depends on the period of time that your schedule covers.

Weekly schedules can include major categories for routine activities, important goals, and milestones, and the deadlines for completing steps toward your goals that take one or more weeks to attain.

Figure 12.1 shows a sample Weekly Control Plan, and Control Builder 12.1 (p. 150) will help you devise a Weekly Control Plan of your own.

Monthly and Yearly Planning

For monthly schedules, list your important objectives and milestones, and the deadlines for completing steps toward your goals that take a month or longer to achieve.

If you were doing a yearly schedule, you would highlight only your major milestones. List the completion dates for your major goals (not the individual steps) and any critical deadlines.

FIGURE 12.1 Sample Weekly Control Plan

TIMES	MONDAY	TUESDAY	WEDNESDAY	THURSDAY	FRIDAY
8:00-9:00 a.m.	WAKE	UP	AND	GET	DRESSED
9:00-10:00	EAT	AND	REVIEW	DAY'S	PLAN
10:00-11:00	Job Club meeting	Workout	Job Club meeting	Workout	Job search
11:00-12:00		Cold calls		Mail résumés	
12:00-1:00 p.m.	Check job board/quick lunch	Lunch	Check job board/quick lunch	Lunch with Sylvia	Job search (cont'd)/ quick lunch
1:00-2:00 2:00-3:00	To library to work on job search	Good time to book interviews, follow up on leads	Good time to book interviews, follow up on leads	Good time to book interviews, follow up on leads	Cheap movie time
3:00-4:00 4:00-5:00 5:00-6:00					Chores at home
6:00-7:00	TIME	TO	DO	RELAXATION,	
7:00-10:00	DINNER,	UNWIND,	WORK	ON	HOBBIES,
10:00-11:30	PLAN	TOMORROW,	PREPARE	FOR	SLEEP

CONTROL 12.1 BUILDER

My Week Ahead

TIMES	MONDAY	TUESDAY	WEDNESDAY	THURSDAY	FRIDAY

Copyright © Carla-Krystin Andrade/Trifolium Books. Permission is granted to reproduce this page for personal use only.

You've become adept at making a routine. Now, think about what it takes to stick to one.

Respect Your Routine

There will be many temptations to stray from your Daily Control Plan, when you will need to use your judgment. But don't confuse flexibility with avoiding your schedule. Stick to your routine by avoiding the following routine-busting traps.

- Avoid naps. Distinguish between real fatigue and boredom or restlessness. Physical activity can combat lethargy and boredom.
- Don't schedule prolonged periods working on one goal or activity. Break your routine into manageable chunks of time.
- Arrange calls and meetings to your own convenience. Use your answering machine, offer to call people back later, negotiate interviews or errands for times that are comfortable for you.
- Keep your priorities in focus. If your time gets squeezed, eliminate one or two lower-priority activities.
- Set deadlines for tasks. Write them into your Daily Control Plan, and try to keep to them.
- If you notice that you're avoiding a job, don't waste any more time. Divide unwieldy jobs into smaller steps. Then begin with the first step.
- Let the people in your life know what your routine is and ask them to respect it. It's helpful to write it out and post it somewhere where everyone can see it.
- Never scrap your routine entirely. When things go wrong, have a backup plan—for example, a shorter version of your list of Things to Do Today. Or identify one thing that you absolutely must do before the end of the day.

What's Next?

Your Daily, Weekly, and Monthly Control Plans will help you take control of your time and job search. Now move on to the chapters of Stage 4: Stay In Control to learn how to make your changes last.

REMEMBER

✔ Long-term planning allows you to keep sight of deadlines and achieve your goals.

✔ Learn to avoid routine-wrecking traps. A routine is useless unless you (and the people in your life) respect it.

STAGE 4

Stay in Control

The chapters of Stage 3 showed you how to apply the principles and practical hints from Stages 1 and 2. By now, you

- Recognize the most common time management traps facing job hunters
- Have begun a Daily Control Plan to overcome these
- Can plan in the short and long term to ensure your job-hunting success.

You've got the basics of the Andrade Method.

While changes such as these can be difficult to initiate, maintaining them can be harder still. Typical blocks to change include

- Difficulty carrying out the daily activities necessary to change
- Lack of support (or outright resistance) from the people in your life
- Your psychological resistance to change.

Yet, you are in control. You can overcome obstacles and make your changes last. The chapters of Stage 4 will help you

- Achieve your goals
- Improve your decision and communication skills
- Create a Personal Support Plan that will benefit your job search and your relationships
- Cultivate an attitude of success
- Stay motivated
- Keep your expectations realistic
- Be patient with yourself as you strive toward meaningful change.

CHAPTER 13

Stay On Track

How has Frank, our job hunter from Chapter 8, maintained the changes he's tried to make in his job search?

"Darn, I've blown it again," groans Frank, rolling out of bed. The clock radio on the other side of the room says 1:30 p.m. Although he has followed his Daily Control Plan diligently for the last two weeks, Frank forgot to set his alarm last night. He feels he's in a slump once more, and isn't sure why. He set some goals, but somehow hasn't gotten organized to achieve any of them. "I'm right back where I started," he grumbles.

Frank has "hit the wall." Why did he falter?

Many job hunters who strive to take control of their situation falter when they

- Lose sight of the main points of a new strategy
- Experience difficulties solving problems
- Neglect to act on their goals
- Fail to communicate clearly with others.

What Frank doesn't know is that such obstacles are not a reason to give up. Rather, they are part of the process of change.

Think of obstacles as a challenge, not a sign of failure. Each time you devise a way to overcome an obstacle to your progress, you increase your skills, reinforce your desired changes, and move closer to your goal.

The Ten Control Principles

The Andrade Method uses Ten Control Principles for staying in charge of your job search. These are listed in Control Builder 13.1. After you have completed this Control Builder, keep a list of your most important Control Principles in a place where you will see them often. Whenever your job search falters, check to see whether you are consistently applying them.

CONTROL 13.1 BUILDER

The Ten Control Principles

Check (✔) the Control Principles that seem most important for you. In the right-hand column, note which problems these Control Principles might help you to overcome. (Use further sheets of paper if necessary.)

Ten Control Principles I Can Use	Problems They Can Help Me Overcome
___ 1. Treat job hunting as my job.	
___ 2. Silence my inner critic.	
___ 3. Maintain my self-respect.	
___ 4. Remember my strengths.	
___ 5. Be good to myself.	
___ 6. Control my stress levels.	
___ 7. Take care of my body.	
___ 8. Know where I'm headed.	
___ 9. Value and control my time.	
___ 10. Have someone on my side.	

Ten Steps to Action

A list of unachieved goals can be as damaging to your self-confidence as not having any goals at all. In Chapter 4, you learned to choose goals that are

- Concrete
- Within your power to achieve
- Realistic
- Important
- Timely
- Positive
- Gratifying to you.

In order to achieve your goals, you need an Action Plan detailing the steps along the way. The Andrade Method takes you from theory to action in ten steps:

- Step 1: Record Your Goal
- Step 2: Make Your Goal Concrete and Specific
- Step 3: How Will You Achieve Your Goal?
- Step 4: Write an Action Plan

- Step 5: Set Your Rewards
- Step 6: Put Aside Time for Your Goal
- Step 7: Stop Planning
- Step 8: Work on Your Goal Each Day
- Step 9: Stay Motivated
- Step 10: Keep Your Plans Realistic.

As Heinz, our job hunter from Chapter 4, uses these steps to put one of his goals into action, consider how you might apply them to a goal of your own. You will then complete an Action Plan of your own in Control Builder 13.2 (pp. 160–162).

Step 1: Record Your Goal

Heinz selected one of the five original goals he recorded:

"My goal is to improve my method of sending out résumés."

If you did not complete Control Builder 4.3: Goals I Want to Achieve (p. 48), do so now. Recording your goals makes it easier to refine them. It also increases your commitment to persevere with them.

Step 2: Make Your Goal Concrete and Specific

Heinz needs to specify his goal and set an approximate deadline for completing it.

"I plan to create a schedule for sending out résumés and a filing system for responses from companies by March 25th."

Step 3: How Will You Achieve Your Goal?

Break down your goal into smaller steps and describe how you intend to achieve each one. Include what you need to learn, as well as any supplies or equipment you may require. If you end up with more than a dozen steps, simplify your plan.

Heinz thought he could improve his résumé system in nine steps:

"1. Design filing system of index cards for company names and job ads and a separate filing system for correspondence.
2. Design three different résumés suitable for the types of jobs I apply for most.
3. Type standard cover and thank-you letters that I can modify for individual companies.
4. Purchase necessary supplies: paper, file folders, stamps, labels.
5. Sketch a timetable for researching new job openings, mailing résumés, and telephone follow-ups.
6. Organize letters already sent to companies.

7. Research new companies.
8. Test the system with a batch of six résumés.
9. See how the system works and refine it."

Step 4: Write an Action Plan

Decide approximately how long each step will take. List the steps in order, setting an approximate date for completing each. Check that completing all the steps won't take longer than your deadline for achieving your goal. The dates you select are guidelines only; you can always modify them.

Heinz wrote his first Action Plan:

"Goal: Fully functioning résumé organization system by March 25th

1. Design and type résumés (1-week goal)
2. Design filing system (1-week goal)
3. Type cover and thank-you letters (2-day goal)
4. Purchase supplies (1-day goal)
5. Sketch mailing schedule (1-day goal)
6. Organize correspondence (2-day goal)
7. Research new companies (2-week goal)
8. Test system (2-week goal)
9. Refine system (1-week goal)
10. System completed (March 25th)."

Step 5: Set Your Rewards

Decide how you will reward yourself for achieving each step, and write this into your Action Plan.

Heinz's rewards:

"• *Each day that I work on my mailing system for two hours, I'll unwind with a chess problem in the evening for half an hour*
• *When my résumés are all organized, I'll reward myself with a movie*
• *When the system is up and running, I'll treat myself to dessert and a capuccino at the Green Bay Café*
• *My further reward will be a more efficient and productive job search."*

Step 6: Put Aside Time for Your Goal

Consult your date book and block off time to work on the first step of your goal. As soon as you've completed the first step, set a time for working on the second.

Heinz made a quick note in his diary:

"Jan. 25th—Spend the afternoon sorting résumés, cover letters, and newspaper clippings into boxes."

Step 7: Stop Planning

At some point, you have to stop planning and start working on your goal. You can always improve your plan later.

Once you've got a basic plan that seems reasonable, take a break—and reward yourself for making a start.

Step 8: Work on Your Goal Each Day

Incorporate your Action Plan into your Daily Control Plan. When you do your night-before planning, check your Action Plan to see where you are in your list of steps towards your goal. Select one step that you can work on the next day, and write it into your Daily Control Plan.

Heinz might incorporate his Action Plan into his Daily Control Plan by scheduling a specific block of time for organizing his correspondence.

Step 9: Stay Motivated

To stay motivated as you work on your goal:

- Post your goal in a place where you can read it daily
- Devise a few positive statements about achieving your goal and repeat them to yourself often
- Visualize yourself successfully completing each step of your goal
- Reward yourself
- Surround yourself with people who support you in your goal.

A few weeks into his Action Plan, Heinz began skipping his résumé-sorting sessions. Here is how he took the situation in hand:

"I decided I wouldn't miss another week. I stuck my Action Plan on the fridge door, with a note to myself to spend at least 10 minutes on it every day. Each time I complained about how tedious the work was, I'd remind myself of all the ways in which the system would improve my job search. And I imagined the finished system landing me my dream job."

Step 10: Keep Your Plans Realistic

Review your Action Plan occasionally to see if it is still feasible. If you can't meet your deadlines, change them.

Heinz revamped his schedule in light of the time he lost during his slow week. This time, he allowed himself longer to work on certain sections.

"Goal: Fully functioning résumé organization system by April 15th

*1. Design and type résumés (1-week goal) ** complete*
*2. Design filing system (1-week goal) ** complete*

3. *Type cover and thank-you letters (2-day goal) ** complete*
4. *Purchase supplies (2-day goal)*
5. *Sketch mailing schedule (2-day goal)*
6. *Organize correspondence (4-day goal)*
7. *Research new companies (2.5-week goal)*
8. *Test system (2.5-week goal)*
9. *Refine system (2-week goal)*
10. *System completed (April 15th)."*

Heinz's Action Plan is a vast improvement over his original vague goal "to improve my method of sending out résumés."

The Ten Steps to Action and Control Builder 13.2: My Action Plan (pp. 160–162) will help you focus your goals and chart your path to success.

Solve Problems Effectively

Make an effort to face obstacles *as they arise* in your job search. Often, simply confronting a problem can reduce your stress levels. But problem solving itself can be stressful.

Common problem-solving pitfalls include

- Feeling overwhelmed by the problem
- Not knowing where to begin to look for a solution
- Inability to make a decision
- Feeling trapped by the decisions you've made.

The Andrade Method uses eight steps in solving problems more effectively.

- Step 1: Be Mentally and Physically Prepared
- Step 2: Clarify the Problem
- Step 3: Explore the Alternatives
- Step 4: Weigh the Alternatives
- Step 5: Identify Your Needs
- Step 6: Don't Compromise Your Values
- Step 7: Make Your Decision
- Step 8: Make the Most of Your Decision

Take the Problem Out of Problem Solving

Marie-Louise is a registered nurse who recently moved to the city. After six months of job hunting, she was low on cash. Taking a temporary job waiting tables at Sam's Bistro was appealing. But it was shift work, and that could pose problems.

Turn to page 162 to see how Marie-Louise might apply the Eight Steps to Effective Problem Solving to her situation.

CONTROL 13.2 BUILDER

My Action Plan

For this exercise, choose any one of your goals from Control Builder 4.3 (p. 48).

Step 1: Record Your Goal
Write your goal here:

____

Step 2: Make Your Goal Concrete and Specific
Decide

- What you hope to gain by achieving this goal
- How long it will take you to achieve it.

Rewrite your goal, making it specific and concrete:

____

____

Step 3: How Will You Achieve Your Goal?
Break your goal down into smaller, manageable steps.

- List all steps, exactly as they occur to you, in column 1, below.
- Estimate how long each step will take and write that in column 2.
- Finally, decide the order in which you want to achieve each step, and place this ranking in column 3.

1. Step	2. How Long Will Each Step Take?	3. In What Order Will I Do Each Step?

Step 4: Write an Action Plan

- In column 1, below, rewrite the steps to your goal in their correct order.
- In column 2, fill in an approximate time or date for completing each step.

Step 5: Set Your Rewards

Select some simple rewards and fill these in column 3, below.

1. Step	2. Date/Time to Complete	3. Reward
1		
2		
3		
4		
5		
6		
7		
8		
9		
10		

Step 6: Put Aside Time for Your Goal

When are you going to begin working on your goal?

Date: ______________ Time: ______________

Step 7: Stop Planning

Decide on a cut-off date for finalizing your plan.

Date: ______________

Step 8: Work On Your Goal Each Day

Steps toward your goal that you can include in your Daily Control Plan are:

Time	Step:
______________	______________
______________	______________
______________	______________
______________	______________

☞

Step 9: Stay Motivated
How will you maintain your enthusiasm until you achieve your goal?

____

____

Step 10: Keep Your Plans Realistic
Update your Action Plan whenever you discover that you cannot stick to your original schedule.

Eight Steps to Effective Problem Solving

Step 1: Be Mentally and Physically Prepared

As far as possible, tackle decisions when you are at your best mentally and physically. If you've had a sleepless night or a stressful day, this may not be the best time to address your problem.

Marie-Louise decided that, after a hectic day of running errands and filling in job applications, she was too exhausted to make a decision about the job at Sam's. In her daytimer, she penciled in some time on Wednesday afternoon, her "free" day, to think about an interim job.

Step 2: Clarify the Problem

Marie-Louise reduced her dilemma to two key questions:

"• *Would working shifts at Sam's leave me with too little time and energy for my job search, and therefore sidetrack me from my goal of working as a pediatric nurse?*
• *If I turn down the job at Sam's, can I survive on a tight budget a while longer?"*

Marie-Louise knew that she wouldn't give up her goal for an interim job. She also did not wish to deplete her savings. However, she was concerned that she could not handle a job search along with shift work.

Step 3: Explore Your Alternatives

By Wednesday evening, Marie-Louise had come up with three possible courses of action:

"• *Refuse the job at Sam's and keep looking for a nursing job*
• *Juggle my job search with the job at Sam's until a nursing job comes along*
• *Work full-time at Sam's for a few weeks and then return to my job search."*

Step 4: Weigh the Alternatives

For each option outlined in step 3, decide the short- and long-term consequences. What are the costs and benefits?

Marie-Louise outlined her costs and benefits:

"• *Refuse the offer at Sam's.*
Advantage: I can concentrate on my job search full time and will have a better chance of getting the job I want.
Disadvantage: I may run out of cash before a job comes along and may have to go home to my parents.

"• *Juggle interim job with job search.*
Advantage: I won't have to worry about money.
Disadvantage: I'll be too exhausted and overextended to do either my job or my job search properly.

"• *Work a few weeks, then quit.*
Advantage: I could build up my savings and would lose only a few weeks from my job search.
Disadvantage: I would lose time from my job search."

Step 5: Identify Your Needs

Making a decision without knowing what you want or need from it may leave you feeling compromised or regretful later. While you may wish to consider how your decision will affect others, it is more important to ask what you need.

Marie-Louise decided that financial stability was important to her. She had been living with uncertain finances for too long, and preferred not to ask her parents for further help.

Step 6: Don't Compromise Your Values

If you want to be able to live with your decision, stick to your beliefs and values. Others may pressure or ridicule you. But this is better than the alternatives—feeling guilty, regretting your decision, or hating yourself for giving in to peer pressure.

Marie-Louise knew that, regardless of the possible benefits, she couldn't lie to the manager of Sam's Bistro about her intention to leave after a few weeks.

Step 7: Make Your Decision

Don't put off making a decision any longer than is necessary. You are deliberating too much if you

- Go over and over the same options without gaining any new insights

- Find the problem is becoming more complicated
- Begin to lose sleep
- Miss crucial deadlines
- Can't remember the decision you were trying to make.

Marie-Louise decided to sleep on her decision. On Thursday morning, she felt more refreshed. She decided that she would work full time for a few weeks, put some money in the bank, and then return to her job search with her mind at ease about her finances.

Step 8: Make the Most of Your Decision

The final step of sound problem solving is learning to live with your decisions and making the best of your choices.

Once she decided to work at Sam's, Marie-Louise stopped deliberating. She drew up a plan for acting on her decision:

"• *Call the manager of Sam's and let him know I am considering the job on a short-term basis only.*
- *If he agrees, tell him I'll begin right away. If not, continue looking for another job."*

Control Builder 13.3: Solve Your Problem will guide you through the Eight Steps to Effective Problem Solving. Quick Tips: Make the Most of Your Decision offers further hints for living with the decisions you make.

Good decision skills will help you overcome the obstacles to your goals. The more problems you solve, the easier the decision process becomes.

Now turn to page 166 to find out how to enhance one of your most important attributes for job-hunting success—your communication skills.

QUICK tips

Make the Most of Your Decision

- Don't rehash past mistakes. Your past decisions were likely the best you could have made given all you knew at the time.
- Stop looking for options. Once you've made a decision, further agonizing will only increase your stress levels and erode your self-confidence.
- Allow yourself to change your mind. If you realize that a decision was poor, don't force yourself to stick to it.
- Make the most of your choices. What new opportunities have come out of the choice that you've made? There is no such thing as a bad decision—it's how you follow up on it that counts.

CONTROL 13.3 BUILDER

Solve Your Problem

Briefly describe the problem you face:

____

Step 1: Be Mentally and Physically Prepared
Is this a good time for you to seek a solution to this problem? If not, complete only steps 2 through 6 for now, and jot down a better time for making your decision:

____

Step 2: Clarify the Problem
Is there an alternative way to view your current problem?

____

____

Step 3: Explore the Alternatives
What options are open to you?

____

____

____

Step 4: Weigh the Alternatives

Option	Benefits	Costs

☞

Step 5: Identify Your Needs
What do you need or want from this situation?

____

____

Step 6: Don't Compromise Your Values
Have you any strong beliefs related to this decision?

____

____

Step 7: Make Your Decision
Which of the options in step 4 aligns best with your needs in step 5?

____

Step 8: Make the Most of Your Decision
How are you going to act on the decision you've just made?

____

____

Communicate Clearly

Good communication is the hallmark of success. This is particularly true in job hunting—where you succeed, for the most part, based on your ability to negotiate interviews, sell yourself convincingly, and bargain with prospective employers for salaries and responsibilities. Your chances of getting the job you want increase dramatically when you are able to say what you mean and to hear what the interviewer is saying.

Four Rules for Clearer Communication

The Andrade Method uses four rules for improving verbal and non-verbal communication:

- Rule 1: Think Before You Speak
- Rule 2: Say What You Mean
- Rule 3: Match Your Body Language to Your Words
- Rule 4: Listen to Others.

How might these rules help Bill, a physician who has just completed his residency in psychiatry, navigate a crucial interview?

> *"You are the most qualified applicant we've had," says the Chief of Staff. "But we can't offer you the position."*
>
> *Bill is stunned. This interview, and the one before it, had gone well. What happened?*

Rule 1: Think Before You Speak

Think about *what* you're going to say before worrying over how you'll say it. To keep your answers on track, ask yourself:

- What is being discussed? What are the main points that you want to get across? Is there a problem that you wish to address?
- What am I feeling? When strong feelings surface, ask yourself whether you are responding to the person or situation at hand, or whether this situation reminds you of something from your past.
- What is my inner critic saying? Self-critical messages can leave you feeling insecure and anxious. Silence the critic within, using the techniques described in Chapter 3.
- What don't I want to talk about? Anticipate the potential danger zones in this conversation—sensitive issues that the interviewer might raise or that you wish to avoid.
- What do I want? Identify what you need from the situation, and what you are not willing to compromise.

At first, Bill doesn't know what to say—so he says nothing and does some quick thinking: "I'm not going to get the position... I feel really confused... Is she turning me down because I have a hearing impairment?... No, that's self-doubt talking... I'd like an explanation. If I'm the most qualified candidate, why won't I get the job?"

Then Bill chooses his words carefully.

Rule 2: Say What You Mean

To improve communication, especially when you must deal with difficult or emotionally charged issues:

- **Be specific.** Stick to the question at hand. Choose one aspect of the issue and stay focused on this as you talk. Don't get pulled off track, even if the other person changes the subject.

  Bill gets straight to the point: "You are hesitant to offer me the position. Yet my qualifications are better than those of my competitors."

- **Express your feelings appropriately.** If you've had an emotional reaction to someone's remarks, or an event that has occurred, let the other person know. One useful response is the "I-statement": "When you said/did X, I felt Y."

  Bill continues: "What you've told me leaves me feeling confused and disappointed. I thought my research experience would make me an asset to your Psychiatry Department."

- **Ask for what you want.** If there is something you want, say so. Give the other person options, but don't leave it up to him or her to decide what you'll get.

  Bill wants an explanation for the Chief's decision, so he asks for one: "I would appreciate your letting me know your concerns about giving me the position."

What happens next?

The Chief of Staff is struck by Bill's frankness. She explains that she recently assumed management of the Psychiatry Department and is dealing with older staff who are resisting the changes she was hired to make. She worries that hiring a very young staff psychiatrist might compound her problems.

After discussing the situation further, the Chief offers to reconsider. For his part, Bill is relieved to know that he didn't blow the interview.

Quick Tips: Avoid Communication Traps offers further suggestions to ensure that you make your point.

Rule 3: Match Your Body Language to Your Words

Much communication occurs non-verbally: your tone of voice, the look on your face, your posture, and your gestures can express more than your words convey. Make your body lan-

QUICK tips

Avoid Communication Traps

Here are some tactics that are guaranteed to bring communication to a halt.

- Blaming the other person.
- Generalizing: Using the phrases, "You always...", "You never...", and "You can't..."
- Refusing to accept responsibility for your actions.
- Bottling up your feelings and saying nothing until you explode with anger.
- Pretending that there isn't a problem when there is.
- Expecting others to guess that you are upset rather than telling them how you feel.
- Interrupting other people's explanations.
- Psychoanalyzing others.
- Ending the conversation once you've had your say.
- Ridiculing others.
- Shouting or trying to intimidate the other person.
- Criticizing others about aspects of themselves that they cannot change.

guage reinforce your verbal message. When speaking to someone:

- Face the person
- Keep your arms uncrossed
- Make eye contact
- Avoid distracting gestures
- Speak in a calm, clear voice.

When someone is speaking to you, signal that you are listening:

- Make eye contact without staring (which can be intimidating)
- Lean slightly toward the person
- Keep your arms uncrossed
- Nod to indicate that you've heard his or her point
- Sit still. Fidgeting—leg crossing, foot or finger tapping—is often interpreted as a sign of boredom.

Getting your point across is only half the story. Two people have not communicated until each has heard what the other has to say.

Rule 4: Listen to Others

Treat the other person as you wish to be treated. Try to see the issue from another's perspective. This will increase your understanding and strengthen the communication between you.

These simple strategies can increase your listening power.

- **Be quiet.** Don't speak until the other person has had a chance to say his piece. Silence your mental arguments also. This is the other person's time to be heard.
- **Put yourself in the other person's place.** Try to see things from her perspective. You may disagree, but at least try to understand her point of view.
- **Don't make assumptions.** If you don't understand what someone has said, ask for clarification. Or, paraphrase what you think he has said. For example, "You're telling me that you're afraid we'll fall behind in our rent if I don't get a job soon."
- **Ask what you can do.** The other person has needs, too. There may be something she wants from you, yet hasn't expressed.

Don't Falter

Once you have your goals in sight, don't let obstacles halt your progress. Your job search will stay on track if you remember the Ten Control Principles, act on your goals, and practice good decision and communication skills.

What's Next?

Don't try to keep your job search on track all by yourself. Chapter 14 shows you how to enlist the support of others.

REMEMBER

- ✔ Remind yourself frequently of your goals, and monitor your progress in achieving them.
- ✔ Draw up an Action Plan for your goals. Make it a part of your Daily Control Plan.
- ✔ Make decisions less daunting with the Eight Steps to Effective Problem Solving.
- ✔ Learn to say what you mean—and to hear what you're being told.

CHAPTER 14

Have Someone on Your Side

Being out of work can strain your relationships with family and friends. Yet, the people closest to you can provide invaluable support at this difficult time. A good support network may also include self-help groups and community services.

Don't face your job search alone. Learn to reach out and ask for the support that you need.

Job Hunting Strains Relationships

"Losing my job was like falling into a black hole," says Derek, a marketing analyst. "My friends from work stopped calling; my other friends are avoiding me. They're embarrassed, I guess, or don't know what to say. I feel like an outcast, like I have a terrible disease. Even being with family is difficult. My wife and I are bickering, the kids are feeling the strain, and last week I had a nasty argument with my dad. I've had it with people! For now, all I care about is finding another job."

Like many job hunters, you may find that you have fewer social contacts now than when you were employed. The people with whom you used to work, go to school, or share activities have gradually slipped out of your life because you have less in common now. Your encounters with others dwindle to impersonal meetings with potential employers or staff at employment agencies and government offices.

Isolation—A Common Problem

Without meaning to, you may add to your own isolation. Perhaps you don't want to take time away from your job search to socialize. Or, you don't enjoy being around people after a tough day of job hunting.

Some job hunters avoid social gatherings because they've grown tired of explaining their status. Others are simply too depressed to want to leave the house. Whatever the reason, these attitudes can trap anyone in a cycle of isolation.

Isolation increases the amount of stress that you experience. Although at times you may want to withdraw, it's important not to become isolated, either physically or emotionally. Now is the time to re-connect with the people in your life.

You can build a base of support that will simultaneously strengthen your job search and your relationships. This involves three steps:

- Step 1: Reach Out to People
- Step 2: Build a Support System
- Step 3: Ask for the Support You Need.

Step 1: Reach Out to People

"I can't cope much longer with your being out of work," Phil's partner Chris yells at him. "I've tried to be sympathetic. I know you were crushed when you lost your job. But all you do now is mope around. You look terrible and you're lousy company. When are you going to get another job?"

"Don't start that again," Phil counters. "I'm doing the best I can."

"But it's been months. Maybe you're too picky. Maybe you should look for different kinds of jobs... The bills are piling up. I can't carry you anymore. I just wish you'd stop feeling sorry for yourself and pull yourself together."

Phil sighs. They've had this argument before.

"I Care for You, But..."

Phil's partner's lack of understanding does not necessarily reflect a lack of concern. These periodic blowups stem from Chris's real worry about Phil's present state and his future.

It's not unusual for people to feel awkward when dealing with someone's job loss or unemployment. If your job search is prolonged, family and friends may begin to fear for your well-being. This fear may express itself in many contradictory ways—impatience or anger at one extreme, aloofness and withdrawal at the other. As tensions build, support and understanding diminish, despite everyone's best intentions.

Drifting Apart?

You may feel that your job search has changed other people's feelings toward you. But it has also changed *you*. It has probably shaken up your identity, self-worth, values, and beliefs.

As a result, you may feel that there is a gulf between you

and the people in your life. As it widens, communication suffers. You drift farther apart, and wonder what went wrong.

Bridge the Gap

How can you bridge this gap? By making the first move toward reconciliation.

There are no rules about who should take the initiative in reestablishing a relationship. Of course, you could find dozens of reasons why the other person should be the one to do it. "What if he rejects me?" "She drifted away; why should I do all the work?" "I'm tired of getting hurt," are the most common.

There is certainly a risk in trying to renew contact with friends and family. But there is also a cost to sitting back passively and letting the distance grow. Why deprive yourself of the possibility of warmth and friendship? If you succeed in bridging that gap, you both stand to gain.

Make the first move—soon. Begin by telling them all the things you think they don't understand about your job search. Control Builder 14.1: I'd Like People to Know... (p. 174) will get you started. While you can't change other people's beliefs, you *can* share your experiences with them. Talking to others about your experience can be the first step in renewing your relationships.

Quick Tips: Bridge the Gap (p. 176) offers further strategies for lessening the distance between you and others.

Step 2: Build a Support System

It's important to establish a solid support system while you're job hunting. People are one of your most valuable resources for staying on track. They can provide social, emotional, and material support that can make your job search less lonely, stressful, and isolating. Why not begin your search for support at home?

Turn to Family and Friends

> *"I couldn't face telling my family I'd been laid off," says Niamat. "I'm a social worker; I should have known better. But I felt sick at the thought that I couldn't support them any more. After all, I sponsored them when they immigrated. For weeks I pretended to go to work every day. Finally, my sister told me they all knew what had happened. I was ashamed for not trusting them. Everyone rallied around me. We drew up a new budget, tightened our belts, and agreed to stick it out. Our nerves get frayed now and then and tempers flare, but we'll see this through together."*

CONTROL 14.1 BUILDER

I'd Like People to Know...

Part 1. Write down the things you would like people to know about your job-search experience. Use further sheets of paper as necessary.

I'd like people to know that job hunting is... (e.g., "having to deal with the humiliation of rejection")

- ______________________________
- ______________________________
- ______________________________

Part 2. Let the people in your life know about these issues. If you feel comfortable talking, set a mutually convenient time to sit down together and clear the air. (You might begin by showing them the list you completed in Part 1.)

I will meet with (name) *on* (date and time) *to discuss these issues:*

____

____

If talking is difficult, suggest watching a film or TV program on unemployment together. Or, give them a book that expresses your views.

Family and friends are valuable resources in your job search. They can

- Share your problems and feelings
- Serve as a sounding board for your ideas
- Offer advice and alternative perspectives on problems
- Nurture and reassure you
- Help you to stay motivated
- Accept and respect you
- Give you affection to counter the hostility you face while looking for work
- Assist financially or materially, such as offer job leads or contacts
- Enrich your life with fun.

Yet, in the turmoil of job hunting, it's easy to become confused about whether friends and family are a support, or simply one more source of stress. Control Builder 14.2 shows you how to turn people stress into support.

CONTROL 14.2 BUILDER

Turn People Stress into Support

You can use the steps of stress control planning from Chapter 6 to turn some of your people stress into support.

1. List your top three stressors involving the people in your life:
•
•
•

2. Use Control Builder 6.2: My Stress Control Plan Worksheet (pp. 80–81) to develop a strategy to overcome each of these stressors and make the relationship more supportive. Or, use the simplified format below.

People Stress	Example	My Situation
Step 1: Situation I find stressful	Arguing with my partner about money	
Step 2: Cues that I'm getting stressed	Headache, tightness in stomach; I become critical	
Step 3: My negative self-talk	I'm not living up to my side of the bargain; (s)he doesn't respect me now that I can't support myself; it's my fault for deciding to quit my job	
Step 4: A positive statement I can repeat	I'm doing my best to find a job and contribute to our finances; (s)he loves and respects me although I'm not working	
Step 5: Stress control strategies I can use before, during, and after this situation	• Tell my best friend how I feel; sort out what I want to say before approaching my partner • Stop myself when I start to get upset; take a deep breath instead of yelling • Take time out when I see that we're arguing; go for a walk to cool off	

QUICK tips

Bridge the Gap

- Before approaching others, ask yourself whether you have dealt with your own awkwardness and embarrassment about your situation.
- Negative self-talk can undermine your relationships. ("She thinks I'm a loser because I don't have a job.") Review Figure 3.2: Common Self-Talk Traps (p. 34).
- As you fill in your Daily Control Plan, include phoning, writing, or visiting friends on your list of Things to Do Today.
- Talk about your job search and how you're doing. Let others know which subjects are off limits. People will take their cue from you.
- Try to be less sensitive to other people's words and actions.
- Respect and care for others.

Don't Overlook Outside Support Systems

Where do you turn for help if you don't have the built-in support of a family?

Marta has raised her two children alone. Lena is in school; Rhona enters kindergarten in another year. Marta juggles interviews with trips to the day-care center and school, dreading her children's unexpected illnesses that force her to stay home.

"I don't have a partner to share the burden," she says. "I don't know where I'd be without my friends and the community services I've found since moving here. A social worker helped me find good, low-cost child care and creative play programs that I can go to with my kids. I use the fax machine and photocopier at the Job Club. My employment counselor is keeping an eye out for a job that will suit my situation. My biggest support is the Single Parent's Network at the community center. We help each other through the ups and downs of raising a family alone."

If you live alone, or have the sole responsibility of raising your family, you may find yourself confronting job loss and your job search without the benefit of family support. But that doesn't mean you have to go through the job-hunting process alone. There are many sources of support in your community that can be as meaningful and helpful as assistance from family and friends.

About Self-Help Groups

You may feel as though you're all alone in your job search. But there are lots of other people in the same situation. Getting together with other job hunters gives you an opportunity to discuss your experiences and learn new ways to tackle challenges. And you get the ego-building chance to offer *your* expertise to people who share your concerns and understand what you're going through.

Job hunters often resist joining self-help or networking groups because of the stereotypes and stigma attached to being unemployed. They mistakenly dismiss such gatherings as therapy groups, or else buy in to damaging stereotypes, such as the belief that you can't benefit from contact with people who are no better off than yourself. If you share any of these beliefs, think again.

Self-help groups for people who are looking for work offer you much more than moral support. They give you access to training programs, equipment, and most important of all, new contacts and leads on jobs. They're worth a try. Look in your telephone book under "community services," or contact a referral agency to find a group near you. Try your public library or your employment office. They will direct you to a local self-help or networking group for the unemployed.

A group doesn't have to be large, formal, or highly organized to be supportive. If formal groups aren't your style, connect with one or two other job hunters on a regular basis.

Professional Support

Professional services have much to offer. Because of their training, professionals can help you understand what you, and the people in your life, are going through. They can also work with you on resolving personal, health, and financial problems in ways that your friends and family may not be able.

Those professionals who specialize in career training can provide you with expert advice on how to enhance your job search. It doesn't have to cost a fortune, either—there are profit and not-for-profit services to choose from.

Figure 14.1 (p. 178) lists a variety of services, some of which are available in your community. Check your telephone directory under "employment," or call your local social service agency for details on how to contact these resources.

Take Inventory of Your Support

For one moment, set aside the problems you are having with the people in your life. Who might be supportive in some way? What help might they offer you? How might they enrich your life?

Control Builder 14.3: My Personal Support Plan (p. 179) will help you take inventory of the help you can get from

Figure 14.1 Community Support Services

People who deal with personal and health concerns	Services that offer training and resources on job-search skills
• Counselors and psychotherapists • Stress specialists • Psychiatrists • Psychologists • Social workers • Health practitioners • Public health nurses • Family service agencies • Credit counseling services • Pastoral counselors and workers • Distress lines	• Employment counselors • Career consultants • Job Clubs • Skills training programs

others. Don't focus only on the adults in your life. Children, pets, and even plants can be a source of comfort. Explore your options in the community, as well.

When you ask for assistance, remember that any relationship is a two-way street. If you ask, be prepared to give. Taking people for granted is a good way to ensure that they don't offer their help in the future.

Step 3: Ask for the Support You Need

Have you lost confidence in people's willingness to be supportive of you? Many job hunters don't get support because they doubt that people will help. They are too embarrassed to ask, or don't communicate clearly what they need. These are major blocks to getting support—and you can change them.

Don't expect people to be mind readers. Don't wait for them to come forward. People may hesitate to offer support because they

- Feel helpless that they can't give you what you really need—a job
- Are afraid to offend by offering assistance
- Don't know what support you need
- Don't want you to feel obligated
- Are so overwhelmed by their own problems that they haven't thought of lending support to someone else
- Feel pressured to solve your problem, give advice, or cheer you up
- Think that they are already demonstrating their support.

Break the stalemate—take the initiative. Go to the people in your life for support. Think beyond what they "should"

CONTROL 14.3 BUILDER

My Personal Support Plan

Source of Support	Support I Would Like	How I Will Ask for Support	How I Will Show My Appreciation
Family members:			
Friends:			
Counseling and health services:			
Job-search services:			
Non-human supports (pets, plants, books, music):			

offer to do for you. Instead, decide how you can ask them for assistance.

In asking for help, you not only benefit yourself. Reaching out gives others the satisfaction of contributing to your life. Don't deprive yourself, or them, of the joy of sharing.

When you ask for help:

- Be specific. Don't say, "I wish you'd help me more." Try, "Would you rehearse with me the night before an interview, so that I will feel calmer?"
- Ask politely—don't demand or grovel.
- If you don't want to feel obligated, exchange skills and resources. This equalizes the situation.
- Share your plans. People are more supportive when they know what's happening.
- Recognize that others may feel stressed as a result of your not having a job. If someone close to you has difficulty coping, offer to find out where they might get support. Ask what support they need. Point out that you are a team and will deal with problems together.

- Let others know they don't have to "fix" your life, cheer you up, or give you advice—that all you want is for them to listen.
- Allow people to give. Don't play the stoic and refuse help when it's offered.

"What If They Say No?"

Some people will—so anticipate that possibility. Even if you are reasonable and clear about the limits of your request, others may still feel overwhelmed by their perception of your situation. Since you cannot control their feelings, responses, or decisions, you must focus on your own.

Asking for support is a sign of strength, not weakness. Recognizing your need and reaching out takes more courage than suffering in silence. Even if people refuse your request for support, you will have grown by the mere act of asking.

Enjoy Social Events and Holidays

Social events and holidays are supposed to be a time for enjoyment and relaxation. Yet, many job hunters dread these occasions.

'Tis the Season to be Jolly, But I'm Not

Holidays lose some of their meaning when you're out of work. For one thing, they're no longer a break from working. They also carry obligations and expectations—gift giving and parties, which can be a source of stress when finances are strained. All things considered, you may not feel very jolly. In fact, other people's holiday cheer may leave you feeling depressed and hopeless.

You don't have to avoid social events and suffer through the holiday season. With a little ingenuity and self-confidence, you too can enjoy the festivities.

- Encourage yourself to get out. You deserve to have fun.
- Build new common ground with old friends from work or school. Find other interests to share.
- Find low-budget ways to socialize: sports, free concerts and lectures, chats over coffee, visiting at each other's home.
- Before you go out, anticipate the awkward questions you may be asked and rehearse answers to them.
- Surround yourself with people whom you consider to be supportive. And be honest with them. If you don't feel up to socializing, let them know.

- Don't talk shop at social events unless you want to. Let people know you'd be happy to talk about your job search at another time.
- Holidays mean more than giving gifts. Explore the other meanings of the holiday season.
- Give gifts that are "priceless": gift certificates for your time or skills; handcrafted presents and cards.
- Allow people to give you gifts without feeling obligated to do something in return immediately.
- Holidays are also meant to be a break from work—so take a holiday from your job search.

If you still feel you're not ready to face the old crowd at a party or during the holiday season, Control Builder 14.4: Respond to Awkward Questions will help you keep even the least tactful people at bay.

CONTROL 14.4 BUILDER

Respond to Awkward Questions

Part 1. List the questions you dread being asked at social events. (Hint: Review Quick Tips: Smashing Stereotypes, page 39.)

- ______________________________________
- ______________________________________
- ______________________________________

Part 2. Try to imagine all the ways you might respond to each of these questions. Jot down whatever comes to mind: serious, tongue-in-cheek, or gracious responses. For example: "Are you still looking for a job?" "Not right now, I'm too busy enjoying the party."

- ______________________________________
- ______________________________________
- ______________________________________

You Don't Have to Be Alone

Job hunting may strain some of your relationships. But don't give up on the people in your life. Instead, break the isolation that can destroy your job search and your self-esteem.

What's Next?

Your Personal Support Plan has strengthened your job search and renewed your faith in people. Now, Chapter 15 will help you renew your faith in yourself.

REMEMBER

- ✔ Social and emotional support can counter the distress and isolation associated with job hunting.
- ✔ If you've drifted away from family and friends, rebuild these relationships. Initiate contact and develop new common ground.
- ✔ Explore the many sources of support within your family, among your friends, and within your community. Ask for what you need.
- ✔ Don't let financial problems and embarrassment dampen your social life. Find the real meaning of holidays and other occasions that you share with the people you love.

C H A P T E R 15

You Can Do It!

Have you got the will to succeed? If you've read this far, it's clear that you want to make changes in your job search and your personal life. But once you have the information you need, what are you going to do with it?

Don't just think about success. Prepare yourself for it in five steps:

- Step 1: Cultivate the Attitude of Success
- Step 2: Anticipate Ups and Downs
- Step 3: Don't Give in to Excuses
- Step 4: Learn from Other People's Successes
- Step 5: Update Your Plan for Change.

Step 1: Cultivate the Attitude of Success

In real estate, the three key factors for success are said to be location, location, and location. In job hunting, the key factors for success are attitude, attitude, and attitude. Make your attitude the attitude of success.

To be a successful job hunter, you need to be:

- **Committed.** Before you can attain any of the other attributes of success, you need to commit yourself to change. If you're half-hearted about your goals, your attempts at change will fail.
- **Persistent.** All success stories share one trait—the drive to succeed despite adversity. Don't give up! Dig deep within yourself to find the courage to continue.
- **Motivated.** There are times when changing your life and job search may seem like tedious work. Don't let the bad days get you down. Stay motivated and enthusiastic by reminding yourself of your goals.
- **Optimistic.** Each negative thought takes you one step backward. Be realistic in your goals and expectations. But don't let "realistic" thinking stifle your optimism.
- **Patient.** Impatience can rob you of your successes. Don't

quit before giving your goals a fair chance. Stick around to collect your rewards.

- **Flexible.** "If it ain't broke, don't fix it." But if it isn't working, don't hesitate to change it. No one is going to give you a medal for persisting at something that you know isn't right for you. Flexibility is critical when you're working towards your goals.
- **Disciplined.** There is no substitute for hard work. Successes that appear to have been achieved overnight were often years in the making. Whether your goal is personal growth and self-knowledge or material success, self-discipline will enable you to achieve it.
- **Focused.** Keep your eye on the ball! Don't get distracted by trivialities—or by trying to achieve many large goals all at once. Set priorities, and keep the big picture in view.
- **Principled.** Don't compromise your beliefs and values in your quest for your goals.

These are the attributes that have guided countless men and women to success in their chosen fields.

How do you acquire these qualities? You already have them. The seeds of a successful attitude are in everyone. You just need to locate and nurture them. Control Builder 15.1: My Attitude of Success will help you assess and cultivate these traits in yourself.

Step 2: Anticipate Ups and Downs

Change is gratifying. Change frees you from the habits in which you've been trapped. Change strengthens and empowers you.

Change is many wonderful things, but "easy" is not necessarily one of them. That doesn't mean that changing yourself must be a tortuous, time-consuming, expensive process. Yet, change doesn't work the way people sometimes expect it to.

Myths About Change

Many people think that

- **If you want to change, you will.** The mere act of reading a self-help book, taking a self-improvement course, or seeing a counselor will not automatically change your life. These activities will provide you with information and support only. *You* change your life by *using* the tools that books, courses, and counselors offer.
- **Change happens quickly.** No single crisis or revelation is enough to jolt you out of your bad habits and problems.

CONTROL 15.1 BUILDER

My Attitude of Success

Trait	Ways I Possess This Trait	Ways I Can Cultivate This Trait
Commitment		
Persistence		
Motivation		
Optimism		
Patience		
Flexibility		
Discipline		
Focus		
Principles		

Part 1. Consider the ways in which you already possess each of the traits of a successful job hunter, and record these in column 2.

Part 2. Now brainstorm ways in which you can strengthen this trait in yourself, and enter these in column 3. Use further sheets of paper as necessary.

Your attitude of success will help you rise to the challenge of making changes in your life and your job search.

Change is more often a gradual, even a quiet process. If you don't follow through with the insights you gain from your crises, you quickly revert to your old patterns.

- **Change is complete the first time you act differently.** The first time you break a bad habit is exciting and gratifying, but this doesn't reprogram you permanently. For any change to take root, you'll have to make a conscious effort to continue your new behavior over weeks, months, or even years.

Ensure your success by preparing for the ups and downs of personal change.

Success—Not Just a Destination

There's a lot of truth in Don Sweetland's remark: "Success is a journey, not a destination."

"I've always been shy and had difficulty introducing myself to people," says Nigel, a bank customer service representative. "My shyness was crippling my job search. But I was determined to overcome it—so I joined a networking group for job hunters. I also bought books on communication, and tried lots of gimmicks: a bright tie, a name tag with a cute slogan on it—a sure-fire conversation starter!... I must have gone to a dozen meetings before I actually worked up the nerve to speak to someone. Finally, I took a real plunge—I agreed to make a three-minute speech to the group. To this day, I can't remember what I said. But it was a turning point for me! I'm still not exactly an extrovert, but I'm pleased with my progress. Who knows? I may become a Toastmaster, yet."

If you are truly changing, each time you stumble you'll understand your errors a little better, and you'll recover from them faster. As you progress, you'll learn to avoid pitfalls, and in time, you'll overcome your old patterns. Eventually, your new changes will become habits, and you'll be hard pressed to remember that you ever acted differently.

Don't expect quick and easy successes. Think of success as a lifetime journey.

Step 3: Don't Give in to Excuses

Along the way, you'll think of dozens of excuses why you shouldn't continue working on the changes you're trying to make. Thinking of excuses is not a problem; giving in to them is. Here are some common excuses people give for avoiding change.

- **"This sounds like a great program. I should try it sometime."**

Procrastination comes in many guises: being too busy to get things done, avoiding activities, or thinking about acting, yet never carrying out your plans. The end result is always the same—you don't achieve your goals and you berate yourself for not doing so.

Avoid this trap. Once you decide that something is worth doing, get started as soon as possible. It doesn't matter how small that first step toward your goal is—just take it.

▪ "I've been like this all my life; what's the point of trying to change now?"

Habits are not permanent. Everyone, regardless of age, sex, or ability, has the capacity for change. Granted, you won't change all your bad habits overnight. But there's nothing to stop you from waking up tomorrow and trying something different.

Make success a habit. Change is within your reach. Give yourself a chance to try it.

▪ "This might work for some people, but not me."

No two job hunters are the same. We all have our unique crises, circumstances, and past experiences. If you believe that a self-improvement program doesn't address your situation, challenge yourself to find something useful in it. Make your uniqueness work *for* you instead of against you.

▪ "I'd love to change, but the people in my life won't let me."

There may be people who don't want you to change because they benefit from the current situation. They may refuse to help you, or they may work against the changes you are trying to make. But they can't stop you from changing. Only you have the power to change yourself; therefore, you are the only one who can stop yourself from changing. If change is important to you, stand your ground.

▪ "I tried to change, but I didn't make any progress."

Simply landing a job is only one indicator of a successful job search. Look around and you'll find yourself surrounded by signs of success. Chances are there are things you can do now that you couldn't do before your job search. Are you better organized? Have you set goals, and are you working towards them? Are your relationships better and more supportive? If you can answer "yes" to any of these, then you have been successful in your job search.

Don't overlook any of your successes, large or small. Control Builder 15.2 (p. 188) will help you keep track of your daily successes.

▪ "I've blown it. What's the point of continuing?"

Perfectionism can provide the perfect excuse for quitting. Don't use mistakes as an easy exit. When things don't go as planned, consider this part of the learning experience—not a sign that your attempts to change are futile. Set standards for yourself. But use them to improve your performance, not undermine it.

CONTROL 15.2 BUILDER

My Daily Success Log

What went well for you today? Great or small, list the actions you took that you thought were successful.

Date	Today's Successes
May 25	*I finally made a list of my job-search goals*

If at first you find it difficult to identify your successes, don't give up. Just jot down the things that you feel good about doing.

- **"This isn't much fun."**

Probably not. But it's not taboo to laugh, smile, or do things that make you feel happy while you're improving your job search.

Maintaining your sense of humor helps you ward off bitterness, cynicism, and depression, and can ensure your success. Research suggests that laughter also has a physiological effect: it triggers endorphin release and other functions that combat chronic stress.

- **"I'm tired of depriving myself. Changing shouldn't have to be painful."**

This is where rewards come in. Have you completed your quota of phone calls and résumé mailings for today? Great; how will you show yourself appreciation for your good work? Don't skimp on rewards; make them small but meaningful, enjoyable, and frequent.

- **"This is too much work. No one told me change would be this difficult."**

There's no way around it. At some point you're going to have to do some hard work. Since you know that, we'll skip the lecture and let you get on with improving your job search.

- **"I don't think I can change."**

As long as you believe that you can't change, you won't. Once you believe you can change, you'll find ways of achieving your goals.

Tell yourself that you can succeed. You may not believe it at first because you've spent too many years convincing yourself otherwise. But if you repeatedly tell yourself that you can change, eventually you'll believe it.

- **"How can I change? I don't have anyone to help me through."**

Don't wait for someone else to cheer you on, or praise you for a job well done. Tell yourself the same things you'd like to hear from other people: "Good interview; you handled those questions really well." "That's a nicely worded cover letter." The best motivation comes from within.

Throughout your job search, you'll find lots of excuses to avoid change. If you anticipate this hurdle, you won't be at a loss when excuses rise to mind. To maintain the changes you've begun:

- **Start small.** Focus on one new task or change at a time. You'll have a greater chance of success.
- **Counter resistance from yourself and others.** Even positive changes produce tensions, and these may be difficult. Anticipating some resistance will help you fight the temptation to slip back into old patterns.
- **Take it slow.** Put aside high expectations. Don't expect to change instantly.

Step 4: Learn from Other People's Successes

Success stories are the stuff of books and movies. Yet, the success stories of your friends, relatives, neighbors, and colleagues can be equally impressive. Success wears many faces, and no success is too small to be of value.

Seek Out Everyday Successes

Actively seek out people who have successfuly landed a job. Stifle the urge to disparage their achievement, or to judge your job-search performance against theirs. Instead, congratulate them and encourage them to talk. People are eager to share the details of their good fortune with an interested listener. You'll be able to profit from their success.

When gathering information on other people's job-search strategies, ask

- How they learned about the jobs they got
- How they promoted themselves and followed up on their initial contacts
- What they did to stay motivated during difficult periods of their job search
- Their advice on pitfalls to avoid, and tips for overcoming these
- Whether they have contacts or sources of information that they will share with you.

Then ask yourself how you might modify their strategies and apply them yourself. Bear in mind that their circumstances and resources differ from yours. Don't expect, or try, to mimic all that they did.

Once you're in the habit of gleaning the clues for success from everyday success stories, you can set your sights higher.

Step 5: Update Your Plan for Change

One of the last steps in the Andrade Method is to follow up on your Personal Plan for Change. Review your responses to Control Builder 1.3 (p. 10) in light of all that you've learned since starting this book. Then complete Control Builder 15.3: My Updated Plan for Change.

What's Next?

The sky is the limit! Dare to make change your pathway to success.

You're in control of your job search and well on the way to landing the job you want. Chapter 16 will show you how to stay in control when that job is yours.

CONTROL 15.3 BUILDER

My Updated Plan for Change

Review the list of items that you targeted for change in Control Builder 1.3. Have any of these changed? Add any other areas of your personal life or job search that you would like to improve.

Date: ____________________

Things that I want to work on now (check them):

___ Improve my self-image

___ Deal with criticism and self-criticism

___ Set and achieve realistic goals

___ Get organized; have more productive and rewarding days

___ Control my stress levels

___ Learn to relax

___ Improve my relationships

___ Prepare myself to return to work

Things that I want to work on that I hadn't noted before:

____

____

When I am going to work on these changes (specify days and times):

____

____

My rewards for working on these changes:

____

____

People who can give me support in making these changes (specify individuals and the type of support you would like from each):

____

____

____

REMEMBER

- ✔ Only you have the power to make changes in your life and your job search.
- ✔ Your attitude will make or break your job search. Make yours the attitude of success.
- ✔ Don't be put off by the difficulties you encounter as you change. They will be outweighed by the rewards your changes will bring.
- ✔ Listen to other people's success stories. Use the lessons in them to further your own success.

STAGE 5

Begin Your New Job

So you've got a job—congratulations! But don't discard this book yet. Use it to make your transition into the work force a smooth one.

The final chapter will show you how to

- Overcome back-to-work anxiety
- Bolster your confidence in the skills you bring to your new job
- Create your successful on-the-job image
- Prepare yourself and others for changes in your roles and responsibilities at work and at home
- Reorganize your routine to accommodate your new schedule
- Set new goals for your future success
- Make the most of your new job.

CHAPTER 16

Make the Most of Your New Job

Congratulations on your new job!

Returning to the work force after your job search brings yet another transition. As your roles, responsibilities, and routine change, don't be caught off guard. Make the transition into your new job a smooth one in three easy steps:

- Step 1: Leave Your Fears Behind
- Step 2: Put Your Best Foot Forward
- Step 3: Look to Your Future.

Step 1: Leave Your Fears Behind

Eduardo's hands shook as he hung up the telephone. This was great news—a permanent accounting position starting on Monday. It would be exciting to work in an office again: new co-workers, new clients, tight deadlines, lots of hustle and bustle—and computers. Eduardo hadn't used them in previous jobs. He'd taken a course a year ago, but lacking a computer at home, hadn't practiced since then. This company probably did most of its accounting on computers. How would he manage? In his interview, he'd mentioned having taken a course; they would expect him to be computer-literate. Should he call the company and tell them he couldn't do the job?

Getting a job offer can be an emotional experience: you feel relief, excitement, elation, pride, self-doubt, uncertainty. Make your emotions work for you. Capitalize on the positive ones, and keep self-defeating emotions in check.

"I'm Not Good Enough"

The initial excitement of a job offer often gives way to a period of anxiety. Suddenly, you may doubt your ability to do the job, or to handle the pressures of working.

An occasional dose of self-doubt can be useful. It reminds you that you are not perfect, and spurs you on to self-improvement. But too much self-doubt can destroy your confidence and leave you too emotionally paralyzed to do your job.

You're Right for the Job

Your future employer chose the best person for the job—you!

You are capable of doing the job you've been offered. You may feel rusty, and you may have to learn new information and acquire new skills. These qualms are a natural and healthy part of your transition into your new job—not a warning that you're not right for it. Adjusting to any new job takes time.

If you're in the clutches of self-doubt, complete Control Builder 16.1: I Deserve This Job.

CONTROL 16.1 BUILDER

I Deserve this Job

1. What negative things does your inner critic have to say about your ability to perform your new job?

- ____________________
- ____________________
- ____________________

2. Which of the following self-talk traps are you are falling into?

___ Exaggerating the situation

___ Putting yourself down

___ Blaming yourself

___ Replaying old messages from your past

___ Worrying unnecessarily

___ Devaluing your achievements

3. Come up with one positive comment to counter each of the negative statements you've listed above. Make sure they are worded positively—e.g., say, "I can perform all the skills I listed on my résumé," not, "I didn't lie about my abilities."

- ____________________
- ____________________
- ____________________

"Is This All There Is?"

It's not unusual to experience a letdown once you're actually in your new job. You may find yourself saying, "Is this all there is?" Disappointment is almost inevitable, especially if your job search has been lengthy.

During your job search, you were probably anxious and excited about returning to the work force. You fantasized what your new job might be like and how your life would improve. Consciously or not, you may have expected this job to solve all the problems you associate with being out of work. It would

- Eliminate your main source of stress
- Reduce financial problems
- Restore your self-confidence and self-respect
- Remove barriers between yourself and your friends and family
- Make your life more interesting.

No Job Can Meet All Your Needs

The list above is a tall order for any job to fill. Essentially, you expect that your new job will give you back your life. But no job will make all your problems disappear. You may also be disappointed that your job isn't all you hoped it would be.

This disappointment isn't a sign that something is wrong, either with your job or with you. It's just part of your transition back into the work force.

Lay to rest all your fears about what your new job will be like and how you will perform in it. These fears can hamper your performance at work and prevent you from enjoying your job. Bear in mind that working, like job hunting, has its ups and downs, advantages and disadvantages. Take them in stride.

Step 2: Put Your Best Foot Forward

You worked hard to get your job search and your life under control. Don't lose that control once you begin your new job. Prepare for new demands instead.

Give Your Self-Confidence a Boost

Chapter 2 showed you how to get your self-esteem into shape. Your self-esteem is just as important to you now that you're working as it was while you were job hunting. It influences your on-the-job performance as much as it shaped your performance in interviews. This includes

- Your attitude towards your job
- Whether you show initiative at work
- How you perform under pressure
- How you interact with co-workers
- Your body language
- Your confidence about your overall performance.

If you've been away from the work force for awhile, or are moving into a new field, your self-confidence may be shaky. Control Builder 16.2: I've Got a Lot to Offer can raise your sagging self-confidence.

Trade In Your Old Image

Control Builder 2.3: Profile of the Successful Job Hunter (p. 20) helped you determine a new, confident image to ensure your job-search success. Now that you're no longer a job hunter, it's time to create a new image. Control Builder 16.3: Profile of the Successful Employee (p. 198) will help you make your on-the-job image as successful as your image as a job hunter.

CONTROL 16.2 BUILDER

I've Got a Lot to Offer

In the spaces below, list all the skills you bring to your new job.

Job-Specific Skills	Personal Attributes	Life Skills	Other Skills

Keep a copy of this list with you at work. Re-read it whenever you feel your confidence waning.

CONTROL 16.3 BUILDER

Profile of the Successful Employee

- What does your employee do at work?

  ____

- How does your employee speak (tone of voice, speed of delivery)?

  ____

- How does your employee dress?

  ____

- How does he/she treat himself/herself?

  ____

- What are your employee's health habits?

  ____

- How does he/she treat others?

  ____

- Does he/she have any other "successful" characteristics?

  ____

Once you have a starting point for deciding how you want to reshape your image, Control Builder 16.4 will help you chisel out your new profile for on-the-job success.

Slip into Your New Roles

When you began your job search, the roles you played at home, within your circle of friends, and in your community probably changed drastically. Now, they are about to change again.

You may find that the people closest to you don't realize the impact that your new job may have on your personal life. Avoid unnecessary friction by talking with them now. Control Builder 16.5 (p. 200) will help you reassess your daily roles and responsibilities.

Build a New Routine

With your new roles and responsibilities, your old Daily Control Plan won't work anymore. You can't just substitute work time for job-search time on your schedule.

In many ways, a work-force routine is easier to establish

CONTROL 16.4 BUILDER

My New On-the-Job Image

Using your replies to Control Builder 16.3, create your new image. (Use further sheets of paper if necessary.)

- Things that I do now that I want to keep as part of my on-the-job image:

  ____

- Things that I want to add to my image:

  ____

- How can I acquire these skills/traits?

  ____

- When am I going to work on developing these attributes?

  ____

- The first step that I am going to take to become a successful employee is to:

  ____

because your new job probably has fixed hours, even if you're doing shift work. But there may be activities that will not fit into your new week. You may have to drop some, and find time for others that are important to you.

Control Builder 16.6 (p. 201) will help you create your back-at-work routine.

New Kid on the Block?

The first few days, or even weeks, in a new job can be awkward, frustrating, and overwhelming. Settling in often means

- Not being able to find your way around the workplace
- Not having any friends at work
- Being ignorant of company politics and the "key players"
- Being unsure of what you're expected to do
- Feeling as though you're under scrutiny
- Worrying about making mistakes.

As you grow more familiar with your new surroundings, the awkwardness will lessen. Meanwhile, bear in mind:

- You aren't expected to know everything about your job. Ask for help if you need it.

CONTROL 16.5 BUILDER

My Roles and Responsibilities

During My Job Search	Ones to Add Now	Ones to Discard Now
At home		
At work		
In my relationships		
In my community		

- Don't be too quick to criticize yourself for your performance. Encourage yourself instead.
- Have realistic expectations of yourself. You will make mistakes at first; it's all part of learning your new job. Be patient.
- You don't have to fit into social circles right away. Take it slow. Get to know one or two people first.
- Resist the temptation to jump right into company politics. Get to know the company's history before you take sides on an issue.
- Be helpful to your co-workers. But don't take on extra responsibilities before you know what your job description entails.

Since people respond to the cues you give them, you can choose the impression you wish to give your co-workers. If you approach them in an open and positive manner, they will respond in kind.

"What If It's a Disaster?"

We all dread on-the-job disasters that could cost us our jobs. Don't let these fears affect your performance at work. Control Builder 16.7: Banish On-the-Job Fears (p. 202) should help you keep your most dreaded catastrophes in perspective.

CONTROL 16.6 BUILDER

My Back-at-Work Routine

Day: ______________________________

Time	Old Routine	New Routine
6:00-7:00 a.m.		
7:00-8:00		
8:00-9:00		
9:00-10:00		
10:00-11:00		
11:00-12:00		
12:00-1:00 p.m.		
1:00-2:00		
2:00-3:00		
3:00-4:00		
4:00-5:00		
5:00-6:00		
6:00-7:00		
7:00-8:00		
8:00-9:00		
9:00-10:00		
10:00-11:00		
11:00-12:00		

How to Fill In Your Back-at-Work Routine

1. Using one of your Daily Control Plans from Control Builder 8.2 (p. 110), jot down the activities that formed your job-hunting day in the "Old Routine" column.

☞

2. Mark your new working hours in the "New Routine" column.
3. Which of your former activities do you wish to keep? If they fit, write them into the "New Routine" column.
4. Which activities from your old routine are no longer necessary? Put a line through them and place an asterisk in these time slots in the "New Routine" column. These are slots that you can use for other activities.
5. What new activities do you want to be part of your new routine? Fit them into your schedule in the free, asterisked slots.
6. Review your new routine. Does it look realistic? Adjust the activities and time slots until they fit.

Try out your new routine and refine it until you are satisfied.

CONTROL 16.7 BUILDER

Banish On-the-Job Fears

1. What is your deepest fear about your new job?

____

____

____

2. Is this situation likely to happen?

____

3. If this did happen, what would be the realistic consequences?

____

____

4. If this situation did arise, how might you prevent it from becoming a disaster?

____

____

____

Once you put your fears on paper, they seem less scary. Now put them aside.

Now that you're settled into your new job, turn your sights to your future.

Step 3: Look to Your Future

Landing this job was the end of your job search, not of your future. It's time to take stock of where you are now, and decide where you want to go from here. At the very least, sketch out what you hope to get from this job.

Set Job-Related Goals

Now that you're back in the workforce, your job-search goals may seem less important. But don't discard goal setting altogether. New goals can help you

- Identify priorities for your work and personal life
- Increase your control over your career and your life
- Stay motivated at work
- Redefine your direction for your future.

You may wish to eliminate some of your former goals in order to work on the new ones that will enable you to make the most of your current job. Record your new goals in Control Builder 16.8 (p. 204).

Make This Job Count

Every job can open doors to other jobs or opportunities. No job is too simple or lowly to be used as a stepping stone to success. Often, how you perform your job, and who you meet while you do so, are more important than the job you hold.

Make the most of your job, even if you've taken it just to pay the rent. The choice is yours: you can simply put in the hours, or you can open up new horizons.

"But, I Don't Like My Job!"

Lorna hated her new job. But she would never admit this to anyone. Not to the members and staff of the Job Club, who reminded her that she was lucky to be working. Not to her friends, who were happy and relieved that she'd found a job. And certainly not to her family, who relied on her salary. Her dissatisfaction was Lorna's guilty secret. She felt trapped. In some ways, this was worse than being out of work. She'd had nothing to lose then, but now she couldn't escape without disappointing people. And she couldn't face another job search.

So, you don't like your new job? After all the energy you've put into your job search, it's often hard to admit to yourself—let alone to others—that your new job isn't what you wanted.

Before you bolt and launch another job search, take a closer look at your job. Even if you choose not to stay, it may offer you some short-term gains.

Having a job offers you

- A change of pace from job hunting
- Opportunities to develop new skills
- A chance to increase your contacts and build a new network

CONTROL 16.8 BUILDER

My New Goals

1. Review the goals you set in Control Builder 4.3: Goals I Want to Achieve (p. 48). Which of these do you still wish to pursue?
2. Now that you've found a job, what further goals do you wish to attain?

Job	
Personal growth	
Finances	
Physical well-being	
Mental health/Emotional well-being	
Spirituality	
Relationships	
Family	
Intellectual pursuits	
Leisure activities	
Other	

3. Select the goal that seems most important to you at this time. Write down three steps you are going to take in the near future to work on this goal.

My goal: ______________________________

Steps I will take to achieve this goal:

- ______________________________
- ______________________________
- ______________________________

- An opportunity to establish current references
- Avenues for an internal job change
- Leads on jobs with other companies
- A new perspective on what you want to achieve (or avoid) in life.

How realistic is it for you to change jobs now? Wait for the normal uneasiness of beginning a new job to subside. Then weigh the pros and cons carefully before you make your decision. Control Builder 16.9 can help you organize your thoughts.

CONTROL 16.9 BUILDER

Is This the Job I Want?

1. List the reasons why this job is not the one you want.

___

___

___

2. Weigh the advantages and disadvantages of staying in this job.

Advantages: What I Can Gain from Staying	Disadvantages: What I Stand to Lose If I Stay

3. Now look at the pros and cons of launching a new job search.

☞

Advantages: What I Gain from Launching a New Job Search	Disadvantages: What I Stand to Lose from Job Hunting Again

Compare your responses to questions 2 and 3. Do the advantages of launching a new job search and the disadvantages of staying in your current job outweigh what you might gain from keeping the job you now have? If so, complete questions 4 through 7.

4. When would be the best time to launch a new job search?

____

5. What will you do to avoid getting another job like this one?

____

6. How will you launch your new job search? Will you continue to work while job hunting?

____

7. Is there anything else you need to consider about changing jobs?

____

Once you have completed this Control Builder, set it aside for a few days. Then re-read your responses to see if they still hold true. Your situation may seem different on another day.

You're Not Stuck

If you hate your job and find it self-defeating or destructive, don't suffer in silence. Don't force yourself to stay because of guilt, fear of admitting that it isn't what you want, or a sense of obligation. You *can* get another job. You got this one, didn't you?

Succeed in Your New Job

Your new job brings new challenges and responsibilities, a new routine, and new expectations for the future. You can make the transition from your job search to the work force a smooth one and pave the way for future success.

What's Next?

You have a lifetime of staying in control ahead of you with the Andrade Method as your ready guide.

Enjoy!

REMEMBER

- ✔ Expect your new job to change your daily roles and responsibilities. Avoid conflict by discussing these changes with the people closest to you.
- ✔ Don't be put off by the anxiety and insecurity that a new job can bring. You deserve your job.
- ✔ You are not expected to know everything about your new job. If you need help, ask for it.
- ✔ This job isn't likely to be your last one. Make it count. And keep your sights set firmly on your future.

List of Control Builders

Bibliography

Andrade, C.-K. (1987). *Remedial Exercise for R.M.T.'s.* Toronto: Kikkawa College.

Basmajian, J. (1984). *Biofeedback—Principles and Practice for Clinicians.* Baltimore: Williams & Wilkins.

Benson, H. (1975). *The Relaxation Response.* New York: Morrow.

Brown, J. (1991). Staying fit and staying well: Physical fitness as a moderator of life stress. *Journal of Personality and Social Psychology 60*(4): 555-561.

Delza, S. (1961). *T'ai Chi Ch'uan: An Ancient Chinese Way of Exercise to Achieve Health and Tranquility.* New York: Simon & Schuster/Cornerstone.

Hauri, P. & Linde, S. (1990). *No More Sleepless Nights.* New York: Wiley.

Jacobson, E. (1938). *Progressive Relaxation.* Chicago: University of Chicago Press.

Jacobson, E. (1934). *You Must Relax.* New York: Pocket Books.

Lazarus, R. & Folkman, S. (1984). *Stress, Appraisal and Coping.* New York: Springer.

Mishra, R. (1974). *Fundamentals of Yoga.* New York: Doubleday/Anchor.

Schultz, J.H. & Luthe, W. (1969). *Autogenic Therapy* (6 vols.). New York: Grune.

Selye, H. (1976). *Stress in Health and Disease.* Reading, MA: Butterworth's.

Seyle, H. (1978). *The Stress of Life.* New York: McGraw-Hill.

Selye, H. (1974). *Stress Without Distress.* New York: J.P. Lippincott.

Vishnudevananda, Swami (1960). *The Complete Illustrated Book of Yoga.* New York: Bell.

Vithaldas, Yogi (1957). *The Yoga System of Health and Relief from Tension.* New York: Simon & Schuster/Cornerstone.

Index